ROUTLEDGE LIBRARY EDITIONS:
WELFARE AND THE STATE

I0131232

Volume 9

AUTOMATIC POVERTY

AUTOMATIC POVERTY

BILL JORDAN

Routledge
Taylor & Francis Group
LONDON AND NEW YORK

First published in 1981 by Routledge & Kegan Paul Ltd

This edition first published in 2019
by Routledge
2 Park Square, Milton Park, Abingdon, Oxon OX14 4RN

and by Routledge
711 Third Avenue, New York, NY 10017

Routledge is an imprint of the Taylor & Francis Group, an informa business

British Library Cataloguing in Publication Data
A catalogue record for this book is available from the British Library

ISBN: 978-1-138-61373-7 (Set)
ISBN: 978-0-429-45813-2 (Set) (ebk)
ISBN: 978-1-138-60065-2 (Volume 9) (hbk)
ISBN: 978-1-138-60070-6 (Volume 9) (pbk)
ISBN: 978-0-429-47079-0 (Volume 9) (ebk)

Publisher's Note
The publisher has gone to great lengths to ensure the quality of this reprint but points out that some imperfections in the original copies may be apparent.

Disclaimer
The publisher has made every effort to trace copyright holders and would welcome correspondence from those they have been unable to trace.

Preface to the reissue

The effects on social and economic life of new technologies, and especially robotics, were debated long before the advent of the 'information revolution'. In this book, I explored the implications for welfare states of the displacement of human labour power from industrial production, at the time when globalisation was beginning to affect employment patterns in the advanced western economies.

At that time, there were still few supporters of the combination of universal, unconditional Basic Incomes for all citizens and a society based on free co-operation between citizens which I advocated in this book. The financial crisis of 2007-8 has stimulated wider support for this vision of the future. For example, Rutger Bregman's *Utopia for Realists and How we Can Get There* (Bloomsbury, 2017) has received an overwhelmingly positive response, and become a best-seller.

This is especially welcome as the alternative – an authoritarian nationalism, which includes coercive measures against poor people claiming social assistance and earnings supplements – has become a widespread phenomenon. It would have been beyond my imagination then to conjure up a figure like Donald J. Trump, or to warn against the rise of right-wing governments in Poland and Hungary, then still state socialist countries in the Soviet style. But it is heartening that the alternatives I canvassed have come to be recognised by many as feasible and desirable, and that this book has been selected by Routledge for its prestigious series.

Automatic poverty

Bill Jordan

Department of Sociology
University of Exeter

Routledge & Kegan Paul
London, Boston and Henley

First published in 1981
by Routledge & Kegan Paul Ltd
39 Store Street, London WC1E 7DD,
9 Park Street, Boston, Mass. 02108, USA and
Broadway House, Newtown Road,
Henley-on-Thames, Oxon RG9 1EN
Set in IBM Press Roman, 10 on 12pt by Columns
and printed in Great Britain by
Billing & Sons Ltd.
Guildford, London, Oxford and Worcester

British Library Cataloguing in Publication Data

Jordan, Bill

Automatic poverty.
1. Great Britain — Economic policy — 1945-
I. Title
330.9'41'0857   HC256.6   80-42212

ISBN 0-7100-0824-4
ISBN 0-7100-0825-2 Pbk

Contents

Acknowledgments   viii

Introduction   ix

Part 1

1 The problem of economic growth   3
  (i) The problem   3
  (ii) Employment, output, incomes and productivity
     in Britain   5
  (iii) Economic theory   14
  (iv) Growth in Britain's competitors   23
  (v) Conclusions   34

2 Social consequences of the problem   37
  (i) Automation and income distribution   37
  (ii) Economic theory   39
  (iii) The 'Ricardo phenomenon' and social policy   45
  (iv) New technology   47
  (v) Conclusions   52

Part 2

3 Economic policy 1964-70   59
  (i) The onset of the 'Ricardo phenomenon'   59
  (ii) The Wilson programme   61
  (iii) The failure of the National Plan of 1965   67

(iv) Consequences of the failure of the Plan   68
(v)   Results of Labour's economic policies   75

4 Economic policy 1970-9   77
   (i)   Heath's attempted expansion   77
   (ii)   The U-turns of the Heath government   80
   (iii) The Labour government 1974-9   84
   (iv)   Policy in the 1970s   91

5 The new Conservatism   95
   (i)   The conversion of the Conservatives   95
   (ii)   Monetarist theories of growth   97
   (iii) The Conservatives in office   100
   (iv)   Economic prospects under the Conservatives   103

Part 3

6 Social policy 1964-70   109
   (i)   Poverty and the Labour government   109
   (ii)   Labour in opposition   110
   (iii)   Labour's social priorities   113
   (iv)   The creation of the Supplementary Benefits
           Commission   115
   (v)   Family poverty   118
   (vi)   Positive discrimination   120
   (vii)   The personal social services: The Seebohm Report   122
   (viii) Conclusion   123

7 Social policy 1970-9   124
   (i)   The expansion of the social services   125
   (ii)   Causes and consequences of the expansion of the
          social services   129
   (iii) Family poverty and the Conservative government   133
   (iv)   The social wage   136
   (v)   Neglect of the social security system   139

8 Social control   143
   (i)   The political definition of social problems   143
   (ii)   Paternalism   145
   (iii) The destruction of the paternalist myth   148

(iv) Family breakup   151
 (v) Child abuse   153
(vi) Juvenile delinquency   155
(vii) Conclusions   157

Part 4

9 The new Conservatives and social policy   161
   (i) The politics of class conflict   161
  (ii) The attack on living standards   164
 (iii) Resisting the attack   167
  (iv) Conclusions   171

10 Alternative futures   173
   (i) Growth and conflict   173
  (ii) Ricardo and Marx   175
 (iii) The social dividend   181
  (iv) Other alternatives   184
   (v) Conclusion   185

  Notes   186

  Index   194

Acknowledgments

I am particularly grateful to my father, Radford Jordan, for the help and encouragement he gave me in the writing of this book. I would also like to thank the following for helpful discussions and criticisms at various stages of its preparation: Bruce Britton, Mark Drakeford, Charlie Jordan, Laurence and Katharine Liddle, Sarah Pelissier, Sally Jordan and Ben Fine. I am very grateful to Lora Ridger for all the hard work she did in typing both a draft version and the final text. Thanks also to Joe and Henry Jordan, for extra assistance.

Introduction

Since the mid-1970s, a right-wing interpretation of Britain's economic problems has gained ground. It traces them to the decline in industrial employment, and the parallel expansion of the social services. This diagnosis of Britain's ills influenced the economic and social policies of the Labour government of 1974-9, but it found its most triumphant expression in the election of the new Conservative government.

This book challenges the theories behind monetarism and social services cuts. I shall argue that unemployment and the decline of the industrial workforce are not so much failures in the British economy as manifestations of a new stage of industrial development which will eventually affect all the other economies of the Western world. In this stage, a highly industrialised country no longer increases its production, but through new technology continues the automation of its productive processes. Under these circumstances, both the number of jobs in productive industry and the income of the working class diminish. All Britain's major economic and social problems can be traced to this phenomenon; neither Keynesian nor monetarist policies provide a solution to it.

In my alternative analysis, I shall mainly use a framework derived from the writings of the nineteenth-century political economist David Ricardo. The radical Right has reinstated Ricardo as an important theorist on economic growth, but it has ignored some very pertinent warnings that he gave about the automation of production. I shall show that Ricardo provides important clues about the origins of economic stagnation and unemployment, and their consequences in class conflict. At the end of the book, I shall relate this analysis to the writings of Karl Marx.

Up to now, my own writing has mainly been about social policy and social work. However, under recent governments it has become evident that social policy cannot meaningfully be separated from economic policy, or the Welfare State from the other institutions of political economy. Any doubts about this that may have persisted in the fog of Labour's administration were quickly swept away by the frosty clarity of the Conservatives in office. Henceforward it will be increasingly important for those who work in the Welfare State to grasp the issues which underlie the political definition of social problems.

However, I hope that this book will also be read by those primarily interested in economic and political issues, as a contribution to the urgent problems that face Britain today. Above all, I hope that I have presented complex economic and social questions in a simple and comprehensible way. At the time of writing, ordinary people in this country are faced with a choice between the discredited Keynesian model of economic management, and abrasive and reactionary monetarist policies. If this book provides no new panacea, it does at least offer an alternative way of understanding the issues.

Part 1

1 The problem of economic growth

(i) The problem

The central argument of this book is that there is a problem of economic growth which has not been recognised or faced, either in theory or in practice. It is a problem about industrial development based on advanced technology, and its social consequences. The clearest indications of the problem have been the consistent failure of the British economy to reach targets set for growth, in spite of improvements in productivity, and high rates of unemployment.

It was in the early 1960s that the problem started to manifest itself. During this period, words like 'productivity' and 'technology' began to be used in political debate. In particular Harold Wilson picked them up and used them as political slogans, promising to accelerate growth by increased productivity based on new technology. He won the 1964 election with a programme based on this promise.

At this time, the 'microelectronic revolution' was in its infancy, but Harold Wilson referred to it as one of the important sources of potential expansion. The economic and social consequences of this entirely new kind of technology, and others associated with it, had not been considered. We are only now in a position to analyse the problems of change based on these revolutionary processes – change which has been taking place for two decades.

Wilson's programme was based on the economic orthodoxies of that period. Since then, there have been heated disputes between two schools of thought – the Keynesians and the monetarists – about the management of growth and the causes of problems associated with new technology. While they relive the economic arguments of the 1930s, we are suffering the effects of phenomena their theories

3

have not properly recognised.

In many ways, the British economy provides a case study of the extreme effects of the problem I shall be discussing. A small island, the first country to industrialise, heavily involved in two world wars, it has been a difficult economy to manage in recent years. The decision to attempt an expansion based on new technology was a logical one, in terms of the economic theory available at the time. The consequences of this attempt now provide us with an opportunity to reassess its wisdom, and to modify theory.

Since the mid-1960s, the number of workers employed in productive industry has been continually falling. Although the decline in the productive workforce has been most marked during recessions (e.g. 1974-5 and 1980), it has also taken place during periods when output has been growing slowly. It is therefore clear that this is a long-term trend, associated with new methods of production. The same trend is reflected in unemployment figures, whose rise has been more dramatic, especially since 1974.

During the same period, productivity (output per person employed) has been steadily increasing. In spite of the failure of industry to achieve targets of investment and growth set in the mid-1960s, the rate of increase in productivity has actually exceeded these targets. This trend reflects technological change — the substitution of automated methods of production for labour-intensive ones. But this new technology has been introduced primarily to save costs, and not to increase output. Hence the effect of new methods has been mainly to reduce the workforce, and not to expand production.

While productive industry has been employing fewer workers, employment in office work, in service jobs and in administration, especially in the public sector, has been increasing. However, the most recent manifestation of technological change — the development of microprocessors for storing and transferring information — will particularly affect employment in precisely these sectors. Microprocessors will replace workers in offices much as machines have replaced workers in factories. It is logical to suppose that at some point in the future all production and most services will be performed by machines. There is every indication that we are moving from a hand-made to a machine-made economy — indeed this is what has been happening since the Industrial Revolution. But orthodox economic theory has only analysed the consequences of this process up to a certain point. It has tended to assume that production will increase as new processes, based on machines, are introduced, so that new employment will constantly replace old jobs, which become uneconomic. However, I shall show that this theory is based on certain assumptions which increasingly do not apply in countries which, like Britain, industrialised during the nineteenth century. Indeed, the introduction of new technology does not necessarily entail growth in the economy; and it certainly does not mean that everyone will become better off.

If my arguments are accepted, they have important implications for every industrialised nation – even for successful and rapidly growing economies like Japan's. However, their clearest indications to date are to be found in Britain, and hence I shall start by illustrating the problem of growth from British experience in the past twenty years.

(ii) Employment, output, incomes and productivity in Britain

(a) Employment

The numbers of workers employed in productive industry in Britain have been declining steadily since 1966, when they reached a peak of 11,852,000. The only exceptions to this general trend have been 1973 and 1977-8, as can be seen from the figures listed in Table 1.1, which also gives their indices.[1]

However, while productive industry was reducing its workforce, certain other forms of employment were increasing. In general these were of two kinds – low-productivity, low-wage work in labour-intensive industries, such as catering; and white-collar jobs (see Table 1.3).[2]

In addition to these trends, there was a tendency for more women to be employed, even when the male workforce was contracting.[3] (This should be seen as parallel with the increase of low-wage work, since women tend to earn much less than men. In 1975 the average earnings of women were only 57 per cent of the average earnings of men. See Table 1.4.)

Unemployment increased more rapidly during periods of recession than periods of expansion (see Table 1.2), but there was a clear long-term trend towards higher unemployment throughout this period. From the figures listed in Tables 1.3 and 1.4 it is clear that when unemployment fell, it was because more low-wage jobs became available.[4]

Table 1.1

	1966	1967	1968	1969	1970	1971	1972	1973	1974	1975	1976	1977	1978	1979	1980 (April)
Number of persons employed in productive industry (thousands)	11,852	11,456	11,254	10,661	10,482	10,092	9,814	9,917	9,897	9,509	9,256	9,310	9,261	9,019	8,631
Index of above (1970 = 100)	103.7	101.9	101.6	101.4	100.0	96.9	94.7	95.8	95.5	91.5	89.3	89.6	88.4	86.0	82.3

Table 1.2

	1966	1967	1968	1969	1970	1971	1972	1973	1974	1975	1976	1977	1978	1979	1980 (June)
Numbers unemployed (thousands)	281	503	542	518	555	724	804	575	542	866	1,332	1,450	1,446	1,344	1,660

Table 1.3

Persons employed in*	1972	1973	1974	1975	1976	1977	1978
Catering	732	794	805	826	850	883	895
Miscellaneous services	1,309	1,359	1,325	1,376	1,449	1,484	1,519
Distributive trades	2,588	2,691	2,707	2,709	2,669	2,682	2,683
Local government	934	960	978	996	958	948	956
Central government	580	583	573	612	623	635	630
Financial, business, professional and scientific services	4,103	4,308	4,484	4,660	4,758	4,778	4,829

*All numbers given in thousands.

Table 1.4

	1972	1973	1974	1975	1976	1977	1978	1979
Women in employment (thousands)	8,331	8,705	8,973	8,951	9,081	9,149	9,318	9,492

(b) Output and incomes

The index of Gross Domestic Product (GDP) at constant prices increased at an average of about 2 per cent per year until 1974 (see Table 1.5), but since then it has increased at an annual average rate of only just over 1 per cent.[5]

However, the output of production industries, having grown at the same rate as GDP until 1973, started to fall that year, and did not regain the same level until 1979 (see Table 1.6). In 1980, output fell again — in June it was lower than it had been in 1975, and almost exactly the same as it had been in 1970.[6]

Average incomes increased even more slowly than output during this period. There are various ways of showing this. Bacon and Eltis have calculated that although the gross earnings of the average male

Table 1.5

	1966	1967	1968	1969	1970	1971	1972	1973	1974	1975	1976	1977	1978	1979
Index of GDP (1970=100)	90.9	92.5	96.4	98.3	100.0	101.5	104.4	110.7	109.6	107.4	108.7	112.4	115.3	117.7

Table 1.6

	1966	1967	1968	1969	1970	1971	1972	1973	1974	1975	1976	1977	1978	1979	1980
Index of production industries (1970=100)	90.6	91.7	97.2	99.9	100.0	100.1	102.3	110.0	106.3	100.6	101.4	105.9	109.5	113.5	100.3

worker increased from £18 to £60.70 between 1963 and 1975, real take-home pay in 1975 was still worth only £17.92 in 1975, compared with £15.05 in 1963.[7] They show this diagrammatically (see Figure 1.1).

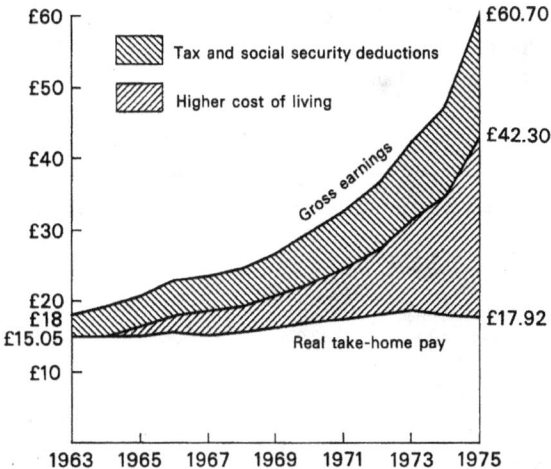

FIGURE 1.1 Gross and net earnings for the average male worker

Total income from employment and self-employment, net income tax and National Insurance contributions, was still lower in 1978 than it had been in 1973, even though Gross National Product (GNP) had begun to rise above its 1973 level between 1975 and 1978 (see Table 1.7).[8]

Table 1.7

	1973	1974	1975	1976	1977	1978
Incomes from employment and self-employment (£m.) less income tax and NI contributions, at 1975 prices	61,701	58,576	55,513	57,069	58,672	61,526
Index of above (1975 = 100)	111.1	105.5	100.0	102.8	105.7	110.8

Another indication of the same trend can be gained by considering the average weekly earnings of manual workers (men) in manufacturing and certain other industries (see Table 1.8). These fell from £60 per week to £54.80 (both at 1975 prices) between 1974 and 1977. During the same period, total taxation and National Insurance contributions rose from £17,079 million to £20,936 million per year (also at 1975 prices). Incomes rose again during 1978 and 1979, but were falling once more in the first half of 1980.[9]

Table 1.8

	1973	1974	1975	1976	1977	1978
Average weekly earnings of manual workers in production industries (£, at 1975 prices)	59.30	60.04	59.58	57.98	54.80	57.99
Total taxation and NI contributions (£m., at 1975 prices)	17.079	18,949	21,922	22,473	20,936	22,360

(c) Productivity

As the numbers employed in productive industry have declined, productivity (output per person employed) has risen steadily (see Table 1.9). 1974 and 1975 were the only years in which productivity did not improve in the production industries. Otherwise it increased almost as much when output was static as when output was rising.[10]

Some of the largest increases in productivity were in industries where the labour force was being most rapidly reduced. Figures 1.2 and 1.3 show the indices of output, employment and output per person employed in two of these — textiles and gas, water and electricity.[11]

Thus since 1966 the general trend of productivity has been upward, while the general trend of productive employment has been downward. Yet in spite of considerable improvements in output per person employed in productive industry, incomes have not risen nearly so rapidly. In fact, during the period 1975-7, productivity in production industries rose by some 8.5 per cent, while incomes fell.

What has been happening, therefore, since the mid-1960s is that new technology has been introduced in the production industries in order to save labour costs rather than to increase output. Machines have been

Table 1.9

	1966	1967	1968	1969	1970	1971	1972
Index out output per person employed in production industries (1970=100)	87.4	90.0	95.7	98.5	100.0	103.3	108.1

Continued

	1973	1974	1975	1976	1977	1978	1979
Index of output per person employed in production industries (1970-100)	114.3	111.3	109.7	113.5	118.6	124.5	128.8

introduced to replace workers rather than to supplement their productive capacity. Thus the productivity of those still employed has been increased, but the number has diminished.

Workers in those industries where new technology has been introduced have generally earned higher wages as a result of increased mechanisation. However, average earnings have risen very little, because these higher-wage earners have become fewer in number. The new jobs that have become available have mostly been in low-paid employment, and these serve to keep average wages down, while widening the gap between the best-paid workers and the lowest paid.

There is no reason why production industries should not continue to substitute machines for workers in this way until production is fully automated; nor is there any reason why output should be increased during the process of automation. If present trends are continued, labour will become a less and less significant factor of production, until very few incomes are distributed by the productive system. These few will be high incomes, but will not compensate for the many incomes lost through mechanisation.

But it is not only in productive industry that substitution of workers by machines will occur. Within the next ten years, microprocessors based on the silicon chip will rapidly replace office employees of all kinds.

New technology does not necessarily reduce employment. If output is expanded rapidly enough, automation can proceed in a way that increases both incomes and employment. In other countries during the same period, productivity has grown by as much as or more than in Britain, but output has increased much more rapidly. For instance, in Japan both productivity and output have grown by over 200 per cent since 1960. New technology has been introduced more rapidly than in Britain, yet employment in production industries has grown.

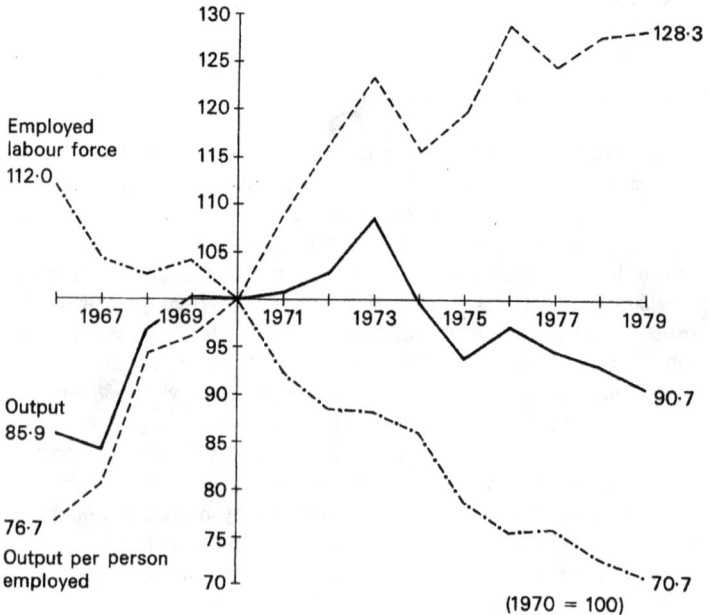

FIGURE 1.2 Indices of output, employment and output per person (Textiles)

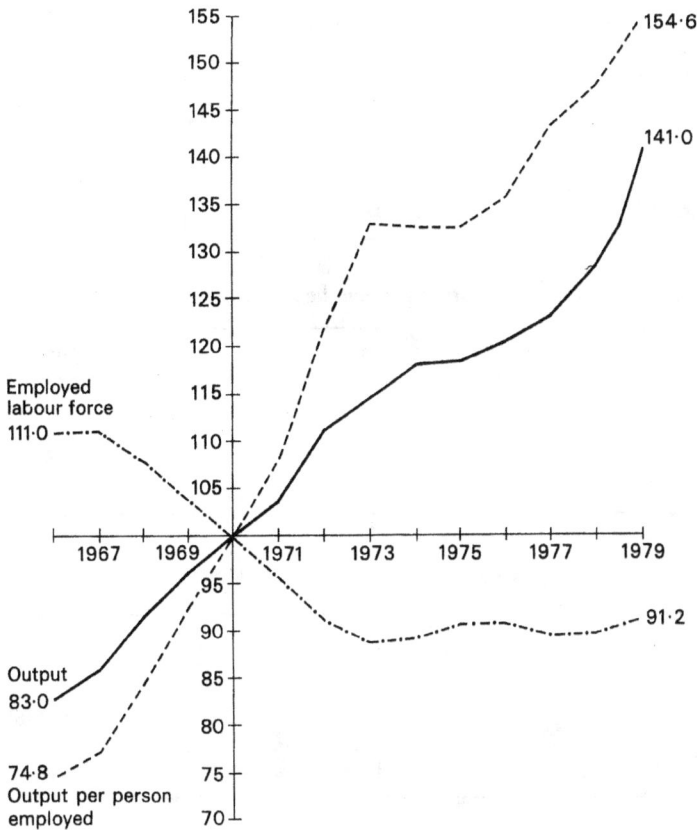

FIGURE 1.3 Indices of output, employment and output per person (gas, electricity and water)

In France, too, productivity has increased faster than in Britain, yet there too the productive workforce grew. Tables 1.10, 1.11 and 1.12 illustrate the different records of the three countries in Gross Domestic Product, productivity and productive employment, in the period up to the crisis over oil prices.

If other countries have combined greater improvements in productivity with a rapid rate of economic growth, and have simultaneously expanded their industrial workforce, why has Britain been unable to

Table 1.10 Gross domestic product at constant market prices[12]

	1961	1974
UK	100	141
France	100	205
Japan	100	315

Table 1.11 Indices of output per man-hour at constant 1963 values[13]

	1961	1975
UK	100	165
France	100	208
Japan	100	319

Table 1.12 Industrial employment (thousands)[14]

	1961	1975
UK	11,989	10,096
France	7,132	8,022
Japan	13,460	18,550

do so? Above all, why has economic growth, the first priority of every government in this period, proved so elusive in Britain?

(iii) Economic theory

In considering the answers to these questions provided by economic theory, I shall pay special attention to the writings of David Ricardo. Although his major work was written in the second decade of the nineteenth century, it has direct relevance to the present situation in Britain for two reasons. First, Ricardo was the first economist to give a systematic account of economic growth in terms of technological change. Second, as Keynesian theory is increasingly discredited, politicians and economists are returning to the models of economic growth that stemmed from Ricardo's original analysis.

Some of the necessary conditions for economic growth were laid down by Ricardo's predecessors, notably David Hume and Adam Smith. In the eighteenth century, Hume argued that one such condition was a steady expansion in the supply of money.[15] Recently, Milton Friedman has argued that no such expansion is necessary — for instance, the American economy grew rapidly in the 1870s and 1880s without any increase in the money supply.[16] J.K. Galbraith has countered this claim by asserting that only the 'hard' money of the eastern states was rigorously controlled in this period; 'soft' money, lent by the fringe banking enterprises of the western states, expanded and contracted rapidly, and was never under government control.[17] Galbraith claims that there is, therefore, no exception to the general rule that growth requires regular additions to the supply of money.

Ricardo's major contribution was in showing how the productivity of labour could be increased by the gradual introduction of more mechanised methods of production. Like other political economists of his day, he considered that the key to economic growth lay in capital accumulating more rapidly than the population grew. Since he thought that profits had an intrinsic tendency to fall over time, and population to rise towards the maximum number that could obtain a subsistence wage from the available capital, the only way in which this could be achieved was through the discovery and introduction of new methods. So long as new technology improved productivity faster than the population grew, real income per person could rise.

Another source of economic growth recognised by Ricardo was the difference in labour productivity between agriculture and manufacturing industry. He assumed that profits in agriculture would fall with the increased use of inferior land, but that employment in industry would increase more rapidly than in agriculture. Since no such law of 'diminishing returns' applied to manufacturing, and the scope for industrialisation seemed unlimited, growth could be achieved by a continuous expansion of manufacturing employment and output.

There seemed to be no long-term reason why new inventions should not continually improve productivity in the manufacturing sector of the economy, but Ricardo sounded one important warning note. While failure to mechanise production sufficiently quickly to keep up with population growth would mean a fall in incomes per head, there could also be problems associated with the excessively *rapid* introduction of mechanical processes of production. In Chapter 31 of the third edition of his *Principles of Political Economy and Taxation* ('On Machinery'), Ricardo wrote, 'I am convinced that the substitution of machinery for human labour is often very injurious to the interests of the class of labourers.'[18]

The way in which this could occur was as follows. There could be short-run circumstances in which capitalists might see mechanisation of production as a means of increasing net revenue (profits) without increasing gross revenue (income). In these circumstances, capitalists would find it profitable to substitute workers with machines, to reduce labour costs. In such a situation 'the same cause which may increase the net revenue of the country may at the same time render the population redundant, and deteriorate the conditions of the labourer.'[19]

Since capitalists were often induced to introduce machinery at a rate advantageous to their interests, but damaging to those of workers, opposition to mechanisation of production by workers was not irrational: 'the opinion entertained by the labouring class, that the employment of machinery is frequently detrimental to their interests, is not founded on prejudice or error, but is conformable to the correct principles of political economy.'[20] If capitalists found that they could increase their profits more (or only increase them at all) by using machinery to save labour costs rather than by expanding output, they would do so, causing a fall in the incomes of the working class, and redundancies.

In spite of these warnings about the possibility of technological unemployment, Ricardo was basically optimistic about the prospect of long-term economic growth and full employment. It was only when mechanisation occurred without increases in output that redundancy resulted; so long as mechanisation increased output, rather than simply increasing profit, then 'the situation of all classes will be improved.'[21] In the long run, mechanisation would increase the demand for labour — both to build machines and to use them — and this would offset technological unemployment. Ricardo thought that over a short period a crucial factor was the speed of introduction of new machinery. While sudden innovation could cause widespread distress, in reality new methods were usually only gradually introduced. He thought that 'the demand for labour will continue to increase with the increase of capital, but not in proportion to its increase; the ratio will necessarily be a diminishing ratio.'[22]

Ricardo's model of growth therefore saw a key role for technology, especially in the industrial sector of production. So long as technological innovation could improve the productivity of labour in manufacturing industry, workers from lower-productivity rural occupations would be drawn into the towns and factories, to earn higher wages. Ricardo was writing in a period when protective tariffs and the Poor Laws tended to keep a surplus of labour in agricultural occupations and rural areas, and he and his fellow political economists were arguing the case for increased prosperity based on more rapid industrialisation. He saw the danger of an excess of rural population, and overmanning in agriculture, as far greater than the risk that industrial expansion would come to a halt.

Indeed, Ricardo's model was based on the notion of a perfectly elastic supply of labour at the subsistence level of wages. Because he assumed that population would automatically grow as wages rose, and that there was a danger that income per head would remain static, or even fall, as a result of population growth, he never analysed in any detail the likely consequences of a slackening in the growth of population, or of industrialisation to the point where no more low-productivity rural jobs existed. He also assumed a highly elastic demand for manufactured goods, both from the increase in home-market consumers, and in exports abroad.

The conditions that Ricardo laid down as necessary for economic growth, and the assumptions he made behind those conditions, can therefore be summarised as follows:

(a) A growing proportion of national income to be devoted to capital formation.
(b) Technological development to improve methods of production.
(c) The existence of a mobile labour force, willing to leave low-productivity, non-industrial work, and to take jobs in mechanised, manufacturing industry.
(d) Population growth, at the time in question providing an infinite supply of labour at subsistence wages.
(e) Elastic demand for manufactured goods, at home and abroad.

Against this the only warnings he gave about the dangers of short-term unemployment and falling wages were in conditions of:

(i) The rapid introduction of new machinery.

(ii) The *substitution* of machines for workers (i.e. the replacement of some of the workforce by mechanical methods).

(iii) These changes taking place without any increase in overall output.

Ricardo was satisfied that most of the conditions (a) to (e) would hold in the long run, whereas conditions (i) to (iii) were only short-run phenomena. If they did occur in one industry, they might well be offset by conditions in another industry; and even if they occurred in several industries simultaneously, the effects they produced would be fairly short-lived, as there would be a tendency towards a new equilibrium of wages and employment levels as profits were reinvested.

What has happened in the British economy in the late 1970s conforms almost exactly to the warning Ricardo gave in his chapter 'On Machinery'. New technology was used to save labour costs, not to expand output, and machines have been substituted for workers. It is therefore worth considering whether this is a short-run phenomenon, as Ricardo suggested, or whether it reflects an important long-term trend. We need therefore to analyse whether the conditions and assumptions he made about long-term growth applied to Britain in this period.

In fact, Ricardo's assumptions and conditions have been becoming increasingly unrealistic for Britain for the past hundred years. In the first place, the supply of cheap industrial labour from a redundant rural peasantry, which was seemingly limitless between 1850 and 1870, began to diminish from that time onwards. In 1850, two-fifths of all farms in Britain were still cultivated by owner-farmers, without hired labour. In the next twenty years, British agriculture mechanised rapidly, and these small units became uneconomic. In 1851, agriculture provided the livelihood of 21.1 per cent of the working population; in 1881, only 12.5 per cent.[23] As larger farmers became prosperous, hundreds of thousands of smallholders left the land and flocked into the cities — a process which is still, in the twentieth century, the ideal recipe for economic growth in industrialising countries.

Second, the rate of increase of Britain's exports of manufactured goods began to decline from about the same date. Between 1820 and 1860, industrial output increased at an annual rate of between 3 and 4 per cent; exports grew at an average rate of 4.4 per cent a year throughout the same period, and continued to grow at the same rate until 1870. Between 1870 and 1890 the annual rate of increase in exports fell to 2.1 per cent, and between 1890 and 1900 to 0.7 per cent.[24]

In about 1870, Britain reached its peak as an exporting nation; ever since then our share of world trade has been diminishing, and the elasticity of overseas demand for our products has been falling.

Indeed, ever since then also the rate at which we have been industrialising has been declining. 1870 was the pinnacle of our success as a manufacturing economy, and our efficiency as a manufacturing nation is therefore in a sense defined, for all time, in 1870 terms. Obviously the process of industrialisation continued from 1870 onwards, but not as rapidly. Physical industrial capital per head rose by 35 per cent between 1865 and 1875, but the rate of growth of industrial output had already begun to decline. Contrary to Ricardo's assumptions, the demand for capital did not rise rapidly after the mid-1870s, and domestic net capital formation was a lower proportion of net national product in the last two decades of the nineteenth century than in the 1870s.

Britain's industrial competitors — first Germany and then the United States — were already beginning in the 1880s and 1890s to take a larger share of world trade. Britain was already starting to be in the painful position of redeploying *industrial* resources of capital and labour — rather than simply absorbing new labour from agriculture into new manufacturing businesses. Clearly this process (about which Ricardo expressed himself in only the most general manner) is a much more difficult one than its historical predecessor. Countries which industrialised later than Britain were at an advantage in competition in growth industries from 1870 onwards, in that they were still absorbing cheap labour form the rural sector, and building new plant, while Britain was already involved in some redeployment of industrial capital and relocation of higher-wage industrial workers.

Once manufacturing industry is established on a large scale, it is far harder to adapt the economy to new patterns of demand than before industrialisation takes place. British industry has often been accused of inefficiency since 1870; the fact is that ever since it has been efficient in 1870 terms. Not only the buildings and plant, but also the towns and cities, the urban life-styles and the population trends were all moulded — with considerable upheaval, stress and suffering — by the rapid process of industrialisation in the century before 1870. Once this process had occurred, no amount of political exhortation could dismantle its industrial, urban and social consequences. Any change was bound to be slower — with wars and bomb destruction being the only obvious external accelerating factors.

The textile industry provides a clear case study of the difficulty of the process of change after industrialisation. Employment in the textile industry has declined throughout the twentieth century. In 1914 there were 710,000 workers in the British cotton industry; in 1979 there were 66,800. The wool industry employed 261,000 workers in 1911; in 1951 there were still 216,000 workers, of whom 170,000 were in West Yorkshire. By 1979 there were only 73,000 in the whole wool industry, 43,000 of whom were in West Yorkshire. The decline in employment has been most rapid in recent years. In cotton, the numbers of workers fell from 109,600 in 1970 — a reduction of 39 per cent in nine years. In wool they reduced from 145,000 in 1971 — a fall in employment of 49 per cent in eight years.[25]

Yet investment in new processes has been heavy. £2,000 million have been invested in the past ten years to make the industry more capital intensive, and productivity has improved at a rate well above average for productive industry in Britain. An example of the capital-labour ratio in a new high-technology spinning-mill in Lancashire is the Carrington Viyella mill at Atherton, where a £6 million mill requires only 95 operatives.[26] Yet the trend is still towards less employment and lower sales, as foreign competition based on cheap labour squeezes the British textile industry more and more.

Thus ever since 1870, Ricardo's assumptions and conditions have been less applicable to the British economy than to the economies of our chief industrial competitors. In the last two decades of the nineteenth century, the proportion of national income devoted to capital formation started to shrink; the labour force began to be less mobile, as a lower proportion of the available workforce was drawn from low-productivity rural occupations; population growth began to slow, and wages, which had already been rising, even in the agricultural sector, continued to grow; demand for our manufactured goods from abroad began to become less elastic. Only technological improvement remained as a factor available for ready exploitation in the search for economic growth.

As a footnote to this section, it is perhaps worth mentioning population as a factor in growth. Nineteenth-century British political economists were uniquely bothered by fears of excessive population increase. For instance, John Stuart Mill considered that the chief threat to growth of incomes was growth of population. He thought that 'the density of population necessary to enable mankind to obtain, in the greatest degree, all the advantages both of co-operation and of social intercourse has, in all the most populous countries, been attained.' 'The cause of . . . decline in profit is the increased cost of maintaining labour, which results from an increase in population and of demand for food, outstripping the advance of agricultural improvement.'[27]

In fact, the British population was increasing fastest when national income was growing most rapidly. The average annual increase in population in the years 1841-61 was 1.3 per cent. Between 1871 and 1881 the average annual increase was 1.4 per cent. Before the First World War the increase was still about 1.1 per cent annually. But by the 1930s the rate of growth of population had dropped to less than 0.5 per cent per year. Far from restraining economic growth it seems that in Britain rapid increase in population went hand in hand with rapid economic expansion. The figures listed in Table 1.13 for the nineteenth century illustrate this point.

Table 1.13 Population of England and Wales

1801	*1851*	*1871*	*1901*
8,890,000	17,928,000	22,712,000	32,528,000

It is in line with Ricardo's theory of growth to assume that an industrialising country requires a fairly rapidly rising population to maximise growth, in order to expand home demand in line with increasing output, and to provide an additional supply of labour. In spite of the fears of the British school of political economists, industrialisation and rapid economic growth were highly correlated in the nineteenth century with population increase in Britain, Germany and the United States.

By contrast, the population of France grew much more slowly in the

Table 1.14 Population of France[28]

1801	*1860*	*1871* *reduced area – without* *Alsace-Lorraine*	*1913*
27,500,000	36,500,000	36,200,000	39,700,000

nineteenth century — indeed Mill commented with approval on the fact that, after the revolution of 1789, French population grew more slowly than that of any other European nation (see Table 1.14).Yet France industrialised much more slowly than Britain or Germany, despite apparently favourable conditions and official encouragement.[29]

> The transformation accomplished in a century was in many ways less complete than that which Germany experienced in the forty years after 1871. In the first half of the century the movement, if examined as a whole dispassionately and statistically, is barely perceptible.

In 1801, 6.25 per cent of Frenchmen lived in towns of over 20,000 inhabitants; in 1851 the proportion was still only 10.5 per cent.

In Germany, population growth was much faster (see Table 1.15), and so was industrialisation. Taking the much smaller unit of towns of over 2,000 inhabitants, only 36.1 per cent of Germans lived in 'urban' areas in 1871, but 60 per cent of them lived in such areas by 1910.

Table 1.15 Population of Germany[30]

1871	1890	1900	1910
41,059,000	49,428,000	56,367,000	64,926,000

In the same period, the population of the United States, the other rapidly industrialising nation of the era, was growing even faster. In the 1880s emigration from Europe to the United States alone was over 5 million, and in the first decade of the twentieth century the annual rate of immigration into the United States exceeded 1 million on three occasions.

These factors are still highly relevant to economic growth. In the period between 1965 and 1974, the difference between the rate of growth of GDP in the United States and in Britain is explainable entirely in terms of population increase. Real income per head of population grew more slowly in the United States than in Britain in that period. Weekly earnings in the United States (outside agriculture) increased by only 5.5 per cent a year, and consumer prices rose by 5.1 per cent a year in the same period, so real wages before tax rose only 0.4 per cent a year. But GDP grew by 40.8 per cent in the United States during these nine years, because the total employed workforce increased by just under 25 per cent in that period.[31] In Britain GDP per person employed increased by 24 per cent at constant prices in the same nine years, an annual rise of 2.7 per cent. Yet GDP itself grew by only 23 per cent. This was because the total workforce in employment fell slightly during this period.

This factor is seldom mentioned in discussions of economic growth, or its absence, in Britain. Yet there has been a remarkable continuity in the fears about the dangers of population increase expressed by political economists of the Ricardo-Mill school ever since the first half of the nineteenth century. The clearest example of this was Sir Keith Joseph's notorious speech in October 1974, when he suggested that the lowest social classes had the highest birth-rate, and that this represented a threat to national progress. Enoch Powell's commentary on the birth-rate amongst Commonwealth immigrants is another example.

By the mid-nineteenth century, French political economists had learnt the utility of population growth for economic expansion, and were drawing the opposite conclusions. M. Colins wrote in 1857, 'The degree of oppression of the masses remaining unchanged, the more proletarians there are in a country, the richer it is.'[32] In direct line with this tradition, M. Debré may be seen on French television today, urging French viewers to keep up the birth-rate in terms as insistent as Mr Powell's are menacing.

(iv) Growth in Britain's competitors

I am suggesting that because Britain was the first country to industrialise, economic growth has been much more problematic for us than for our competitiors since the late nineteenth century. For many years after 1870, Britain was the most industrialised country in the world. Workers continued to be absorbed from agriculture into industrial jobs for some time after 1870, but the change was far slower. By the 1930s it had slowed almost to a stop. The Second World War and the post-war boom produced a new round of change, and the industrial workforce grew again. However, since the mid-1960s the industrial workforce has been continuously contracting. The numbers of workers employed in agriculture have also been falling, but the only increases in employment have been in non-industrial jobs. (See section ii.)

Among our competitors, only Germany was as industrialised as we were by 1960. The United States, for example, was still a far more rural country; so was France; and even more markedly, so was Japan. Consequently, in all these countries a process of industrialisation much more comparable with ours in the nineteenth and early twentieth centuries was still under way. Workers from low-paid agricultural occupations were still being absorbed in large numbers into new industries, as new industrialisation and urbanisation took place.

Germany's economic growth since the war was enabled largely by the wholesale destruction of industrial plant by allied bombing during the Second World War. This required a sustained rebuilding of industry, which carried Germany beyond our level of prosperity. It also contributed to Germany's ability to continue to expand its share of world trade. By contrast, Japan's economic miracle consisted in the introduction of new, high-technology industry into a largely undeveloped economy. Thus differing rates of economic growth in recent years can be explained in terms of the stage of industrial development reached by each nation.

This analysis leaves some important questions unanswered. First, it does not attempt to consider whether growth of national income is itself necessarily desirable, or should be given high priority. There are strong arguments to suggest that the maximisation of growth does not lead to expansion of output of the most socially useful products, or improve the quality of life. However, at this stage I do not propose to discuss this question. My purpose is simply to analyse why, given that all industrialised and industrialising countries have been seeking economic growth, some have been much more successful than others.

Second, I am for the moment arguing as if all countries were in competition with each other to achieve expansion. Clearly this is not always true, and some countries have mutual arrangements (such as the European Economic Community) in which they have some limited co-operation in an attempt to produce faster growth for all.

Third, I am not considering the question of which countries become industrialising countries, and which do not. The world economy contains some nations which are already quite highly industrialised, some which are industrialising rapidly, and many which remain backward and extremely poor. The latter group are often prevented from having any share in the growing affluence of the other groups by their position as economic dependants on the richer nations. But, as I shall show, this exploitation by rich countries of poor ones does not preclude rapid industrialisation once the latter achieve a degree of economic and political independence.

However, setting aside these important considerations, I want to turn now to the question of comparative economic growth in industrialised and industrialising countries in the Western world. In particular, I shall argue that Britain's failure to achieve significant growth in recent years is better understood in terms of its historical stage of industrial development than in terms of any other economic factor, and that other countries will eventually encounter the same problems that we have experienced. In the world of international capitalism, multinational corporations tend to expand production most where labour is cheaper and relatively unorganised, and industrial development is less controlled and planned. Hence new industries, producing new products, and using new technology, spring up more rapidly in industrialising countries than in highly industrialised ones. Countries which are industrialising at present do not have to pass through all the stages of nineteenth-century industrialisation, but can expand through new developments, like microelectronics.

This interpretation is not in line with the one most commonly made by economists, and largely adopted by the leadership of both major British political parties. The trends noted in section (ii) of this chapter have been identified by economists, but they have not been related to the phenomena that Ricardo analysed in his chapter 'On Machinery'. They have therefore not been recognised as representing an important and universal problem of economic growth based on technological change.

In this section I shall concentrate on the analysis of these phenomena provided by Bacon and Eltis in their book *Britain's Economic Problem*, whose subtitle, *Too Few Producers*, reveals their diagnosis. I have chosen this book (first published in 1976) both because of its influence on official thinking, and because it makes international comparisons against which I can test the alternative model which I have been suggesting.

Bacon and Eltis note that Britain's growth rate fell from the mid-1960s onwards, but that industrial productivity increased more rapidly from the same date. Comparing Britain's economic performance with that of other countries, they remark that our improvement in productivity was by no means outstanding for those particular years, but 'was still exceedingly high by historical standards, and could have led to the "economic miracle" that so many have expected for so long.'[33] They conclude that this did not occur because of low rates of industrial investment.[34]

> In a successful economy all the workers who are made redundant
> by productivity growth and technical advance get jobs producing
> the new and better goods or jobs that result from expanded pro-
> duction of the old goods, but the production of all these new jobs
> requires investment; and net investment in industry has fallen by
> one quarter in Britain since 1965. *Hence, unemployment in Britain
> has suffered from technical progress instead of gaining from it*.
> (Their italics)

Yet, as I shall show in Chapters 3 and 4, British governments of both parties gave top priority to the expansion of industry, and to higher investment. The Wilson government succeeded in increasing the proportion of national income going to investment in its early years in office, yet growth slowed down instead of accelerating. What then was Bacon and Eltis's explanation of this failure?

They argue throughout their book that government policy stifled investment. First, they accuse governments of holding down profits by prices and incomes controls. Second, they reproach governments for using up national resources by rapid expansion of the public sector:[35]

> successive governments have allowed large numbers of workers to
> move out of industry and into various service occupations, where
> they still consume and invest industrial products, but produce none
> themselves . . . the proportion of the nation's labour force that has
> been producing marketed output has been falling year by year; at
> the same time those who have had to rely on others to produce
> marketed output for them, civil servants, social workers and most
> teachers and medical workers, have been increasingly numerous,
> and they have had to satisfy their requirements by consuming goods
> and services that diminishing numbers of market-sector workers
> are producing.

Hence Bacon and Eltis suggest that Britain's problem started when investment began to fall and the public sector began to grow. But the causal links in their argument rest on a very improbable series of government decisions. They invite us to suppose that governments committed to growth chose to restrict profits and expand the social services just when an economic miracle was becoming possible for the first time since the war; that the Wilson government, which made industrial investment and new technology its slogan decided to stifle their growth at the very moment that its policies were beginning to succeed; and that the Heath government, pledged to control public spending, cheerfully ate up profits by creating extravagant social services. The truth, as I shall show in later chapters, is that by the late 1960s higher investment was already failing to produce higher output or new employment, and that the Heath government only expanded social service expenditure after every other effort to produce new jobs had failed.

Bacon and Eltis assume in their analysis that higher rates of industrial investment always lead to higher rates of growth. Ricardo showed that more investment could simply lead to the more rapid replacement of workers by machines, without higher output, unless certain other conditions existed. The international comparisons provided by Bacon and Eltis themselves illustrate this point. In what follows I shall use their figures, since they relate to the period up to the crisis over oil prices, which has since complicated the picture slightly, exaggerating trends that were present previously.

If Bacon and Eltis's arguments held good, there would be a simple and direct correlation between high rates of investment and high rates of growth. There is some correlation during the period in question, but the exceptions are highly significant. For example, the share of gross investment in GDP was significantly lower in the United States than in Britain between 1961 and 1974. In Britain the proportions were 0.173 in 1961 and 0.205 in 1974; in the United States they were 0.163 and 0.175. If market sector investment (which Bacon and Eltis consider crucial) is compared, net investment was about twice as high in Britain as in the United States in the 1970s. In 1975, market sector investment took 5.3 per cent of marketed output in Britain, and only 2.5 per cent in the United States. Yet in Britain, GDP grew by only 41 per cent in this period, and in the United States it grew by 67 per cent.[36]

The total volume of investment as a proportion of GDP in West Germany and in France during this period was almost identical. Yet Germany's rate of growth was slower than France's — 72 per cent as compared with 105 per cent. We are therefore forced to consider some possible explanations of why investment produces faster rates of growth in some countries than in others. I shall show that Bacon and Eltis's figures suggest that the stage a country has reached in its process of industrialisation is the key to explaining this variation.

Table 1.16   Ratio of industrial to non-industrial employment (numbers employed given in thousands)

Country	Year	Industrial	Non-industrial (less agriculture)	Agriculture	Industrial as a percentage of non-industrial and agriculture
UK	1961	11,989	11,624	972	95.2
	1975	10,096	13,812	667	69.7
W. Germany	1961	12,965	9,824	3,449	97.7
	1975	11,460	11,546	1,822	85.7
France	1961	7,132	7,540	4,044	61.6
	1975	8,022	10,391	2,351	63.0
USA	1961	21,564	38,982	5,200	48.8
	1975	24,565	56,837	3,381	40.8
Italy	1961	7,646	6,155	6,207	61.9
	1975	8,305	7,549	2,964	78.7
Japan	1961	13,460	18,490	13,030	42.7
	1975	18,550	26,650	6,580	55.8

The statistics set out in Table 1.16, taken from Bacon and Eltis's book, indicate the different levels of industrial development between a number of major Western nations, as reflected in the proportions of workers unemployed in the industrial sector of the economy.[37]

What Bacon and Eltis seek to show from these figures is that in Britain between 1961 and 1975 there was a uniquely rapid transfer in employment from industrial to non-industrial jobs. They call this process 'de-industrialisation', and it forms the basis of their argument that our problem is that we have 'too few producers'. They calculate that the change in the ratio of non-industrial to industrial employment in Britain was 41 per cent, which was higher than any other country. In West Germany the percentage change in the same direction was 32.8 per cent; in the United States 27.9 per cent; in France 22.5 per cent; in Italy 12.6 per cent; and in Japan only 4.5 per cent.

Yet this rank order is immediately indicative of the theory that I am advancing. In 1961, Britain had the highest proportion of industrial workers as compared with agricultural workers, an indication that it has progressed further towards industrialisation. The other nations followed Britain in almost exactly the rank order suggested by Bacon and Eltis's figures. The size of increase in the rates of non-industrial to industrial employment followed the order of their relative industrialisation in 1961 much more closely than it followed the order of their relative levels of investment. This is indicated in Table 1.17.[38]

Table 1.17

Country	Percentage change in ratio of non-industrial to indus- employment (1961-5)	Industrial workers as a per- centage of agricultural workers in 1961	Share of gross capital formation in GDP (1961)
UK	41.0	1233	0.173
W. Germany	32.8	375	0.252
USA	27.9	414	0.163
France	22.5	176	0.215
Italy	12.6	123	0.278
Japan	4.5	103	0.343

Thus it can be seen that Germany, in spite of a far higher level of investment in 1961 than France, still had a much greater increase in the ratio of non-industrial to industrial jobs. Italy's rate of investment was only slightly above Germany's, yet its increase in the ratio of non-industrial employment was much less — only slightly over one-third of Germany's. The United States had a lower rate of investment than Britain, but its change in the ratio of employment in non-industrial jobs was much lower.

This indicates that less industrialised countries provided more profitable opportunities for industrial expansion through new investment than older, long-established industrial nations. Those countries which could still take advantage of the large gap in relative productivity between the peasant sector and the high-technology industrial sector could produce high rates of growth. Those which, like Britain, already possessed a highly mechanised agricultural system, with very little manpower, had to redeploy industrial resources, with far less spectacular results.

Yet Bacon and Eltis's figures show that even in the most industrially successful economies there was a considerable increase in non-industrial jobs, other than those in agriculture, between 1961 and 1975. In fact the increase in this type of employment was far greater in Japan than in Britain. In Japan, non-industrial employment (exclusive of agriculture) increased by 44 per cent. In Britain it increased by only 19 per cent. Yet Japan's rate of growth of GDP was 215 per cent, and Britain's was only 41 per cent. This was clearly related to Japan's backward state of industrial development in 1961, compared with Britain's.

It should also be noted that both Japan and the United States had far higher proportions of non-industrial workers at the start of the period than Britain. In 1961, Britain had more industrial than non-industrial workers, whereas Japan and the United States had 72.8 per cent and 55.3 per cent as many industrial as non-industrial workers respectively, excluding agriculture. Thus Britain started from a far lower base-line of non-industrial employment, as well as a higher base-line of industrial employment. Yet Japan and the United States increased non-industrial employment by 44 per cent and 46 per cent respectively, compared with Britain's 19 per cent. This is a totally different picture from the one Bacon and Eltis's argument would lead us to imagine, even though it is based on their own statistics.

Next, it should be recognised that although agricultural employment declined in every country, it declined much more in those countries which still had a large agricultural sector in 1961. For instance, in Japan, where agriculture provided 40.8 per cent of all employment in 1961, this diminished by 49.5 per cent between 1961 and 1975. In Italy, where it gave 45 per cent of all employment, it fell by 52.2 per cent in the same period. In France, where 27.6 per cent of all workers were in agriculture in 1961, agricultural jobs were reduced by 41.8 per cent. Even Germany, where only 15.1 per cent of workers were in agriculture, had a reduction of 47.2 per cent in this type of employment. But in Britain, where only 4.1 per cent of the employed workforce were in agriculture in 1961, the fall was only 31.4 per cent. This indicates that the scope for redeploying labour from rural to industrial employment was much less in Britain than in her competitors' economies.

However, it does not give the whole picture. In countries with largely peasant agriculture, with very low rates of farm mechanisation, and consequent low productivity, the scope for growth was enormous. Agriculture itself could expand its output rapidly through new machinery. But also workers absorbed into non-industrial as well as industrial employment could earn higher incomes, and add to the growth of GDP. In Britain, agricultural productivity was already high, and workers leaving the land could not achieve the large increases of earnings to be gained in peasant countries in the process of adopting modern urban life-styles, such as Japan.

Even so, Bacon and Eltis's figures do show that one of the most

Table 1.18

Country	Agricultural workforce as a percentage of industrial workforce in 1961	Total percentage growth of GDP 1961-74 (at 1963 prices)
Japan	96.8	215
Italy	81.2	83
France	56.7	105
W. Germany	26.6	72
USA	24.1	67
UK	8.1	41

reliable indicators of economic growth potential in 1961 was quite simply the size of the agricultural workforce as a percentage of industrial employment. The figures given in Table 1.18 indicate how closely rates of growth reflected the relative proportions of rural employment in the various countries in question.[39]

The only exception to the general pattern is Italy, where the picture is complicated by the contrast between the advanced industrialised North of the country and the backward rural South. Unlike Japan, which is a compact island economy, Italy presents geographical barriers to mobility between rural and urban sectors of the economy. Even so, its rate of investment was higher in 1961 than any other country except Japan, and only France among the nations with a smaller agricultural workforce achieved a faster rate of growth.

As a final comment in this section on Bacon and Eltis's arguments, it should be noted that Britain was not the only country in this period to experience 'de-industrialisation'. In Germany, a highly successful economy, the industrial workforce fell in this period. In general, countries with a low proportion of industrial workers in 1961 had the highest rates of growth of industrial employment, and the countries with the highest rates of industrial workers (Britain and Germany) both experienced a fall in the industrial workforce. In other words, the countries which were least industrialised in 1961 had the most rapid industrialisation, and those furthest on in the process experienced what Bacon and Eltis call 'de-industrialisation'. But the example of Germany indicates that what was actually occurring was simply the automation of production. Even where industrial output was growing rapidly, as it was there, industrial employment fell because new technology meant that fewer workers were required, even for this higher output. But in Japan, where a whole new process of industrialisation was occurring, new technology led to more industrial employment. The figures given in Table 1.19 illustrate this.

Table 1.19

Country	Percentage of workforce employed in industrial jobs in 1961	Percentage increase or reduction of industrial workforce 1961-75
UK	48.8	− 15.8
W. Germany	49.4	− 11.6
Italy	38.2	+ 7.9
France	38.1	+ 11.1
USA	32.8	+ 12.2
Japan	29.9	+ 27.5

British readers may doubt the validity of these conclusions simply because of their indoctrination in the virtues of our competitors. If the Japanese are more successful, so we have repeatedly been told, it is because they work harder and are cleverer in matters of commerce. They also spend far less on social services. I shall therefore conclude this section by quoting two examples not used by Bacon and Eltis, which raise no stereotypes of industriousness and commercial acumen — Ireland and Liechtenstein.

Not many Englishmen consider that the Irish are exceptionally hard-working or have special business talents, so it must indeed be an iron law of economics that has enabled Ireland to achieve a far faster rate of growth than Britain in recent years. That law is quite simple, and exactly the one I have been illustrating. In 1961, there were over 400,000 agricultural workers in Ireland, and less than 300,000 industrial workers.[40] In other words, agriculture still employed one-third more people than industry. By 1975, the numbers in agriculture had shrunk to 250,000; the numbers in industry had risen to 360,000, and industrial production was still growing at an annual rate of between 8 and 9 per cent between 1975 and 1977, when its British counterpart was declining.[41] Between 1970 and 1976, GNP grew by 21.4 per cent, an average rate of 3.5 per cent per year, despite the recession of 1974-5.[42] Industrial production provided 37.3 per cent of national income in 1976, compared with only 23.0 per cent in 1970.[43] In the same six years, Gross Domestic Capital Formation grew by 19 per cent.

It is ironical that Ireland can attribute its present success to Britain's exploitation of its dependent agricultural status in the nineteenth century. Having been held down in backward poverty while Britain industrialised, Ireland was in a position to grow to prosperity during the period when the British economy was ceasing to expand. The most poignant contrast is with Northern Ireland, which was industrialised by Britain, and consequently considered worth retaining as part of the UK. In Northern Ireland the agricultural sector employs only 25 per cent of the number of workers employed in industry,[44] but the industrial workforce is steadily declining, and the unemployment rate rose from 5.2 per cent in 1974 to 12.6 per cent in 1977. The contrast between the growing prosperity of the South and the progressive impoverishment of the North gives another twist to Ireland's bitter and tangled history.

If Ireland's success is ironical, Liechtenstein's is improbable. It occupies an area of 160 square kilometres, of which 60 per cent is mountainous; it has virtually no raw materials, and was described in the early nineteenth century as 'possibly the poorest country in the world'. Before the Second World War, it was still an Alpine Ruritania, living on pastoral farming and season work abroad. But today its population of 25,340 inhabitants is (to quote a *Financial Times* survey)[45]

> one of the richest in the world. . . . By any standards the tiny
> nation is one of the most highly industrialised in the world. . . .
> Taking industrial output as to be almost synonymous with exports
> in such a miniscule nation, sales to foreign markets more than
> doubled in the first half of the 1960s, then more than tripled again
> by 1975. It has risen at an average annual rate of nearly 10 per cent
> since.

This makes Liechtenstein an even more successful country than Japan in terms of economic growth, and suggests that industrial expansion has very little to do with oriental ingenuity.

(v) Conclusions

If my analysis so far is accepted, it suggests that Britain's quest for economic growth since the mid-1960s has largely been a vain one. Policies which have tried to promote growth have tended to make things worse. Britain's failure in this respect is a direct consequence of our success in the nineteenth century. The fact that we cannot achieve growth, even though we taught the world capitalism, should perhaps be considered in much the same light as our defeats in the football field by countries we taught football, or on the cricket field by descendents of our West Indian slaves.

The explanation I have put forward for our failure to achieve significant growth is the difficulty of redeploying industrial resources of labour and capital to meet changes in demand. In a highly industrialised state like Britain, which has for many years been suffering a decline in its share of world trade, and whose population is growing only slowly, total demand for manufactured goods is inelastic, though demand for specific manufactures fluctuates fairly quickly. New industry is unlikely to spring up rapidly to meet a sudden increase in demand for a particular product, or to start making a new product — as it can in less industrialised countries. Conversely, old and declining industries run down slowly and painfully after a fall in demand for their products.

I cannot claim to have developed a theory which completely explains when or how stagnation begins. However, it seems clear to me that this is determined by some or all of the factors that Ricardo identified. I do not know of a single instance of a country achieving sustained and significant economic growth without *either* a growing export market, *or* significant population growth, *or* the absorption of a rural population into urban employment. Rapid economic growth seems to be associated with all three factors occurring in an industrialising country.

At a certain point in the history of a nation's industrialisation, a watershed is reached. My hypothesis is that in a highly industrialised country, so long as an annual growth rate of above 2 per cent can be maintained, decision-makers in productive industry tend to aim for higher output, and to use new technology to expand production. However, once the rate of growth of the economy falls below 2 per cent a year (as it started to do in Britain in the late 1960s) then decision-makers plan to use new technology primarily to save labour costs, and not to increase output. So long as total demand shows no evidence of increasing, once long-term planning of this kind develops, it is very difficult to alter a trend towards lower levels of employment in productive industry. Productivity increases, but output does not.

During the period of industrialisation, mechanisation of industry increases the relative amount of capital used in production, and reduces the relative amount of labour. However, as long as output increases, demand for labour continues to expand, and new technology thus increases employment. Once the watershed is passed, a new stage is reached. Automation entails a reduction in the demand for labour, so new technology diminishes employment in productive industry. Britain has been the first nation to experience this phenomenon of *absolute* (as opposed to relative) automation.

Once this stage is reached, attempts to improve the rate of growth by increased investment, to improve productivity, fail (as they did in the 1960s in Britain) because extra investment is used to substitute machines for workers, and accelerate redundancies. As unemployment rises, government increases public expenditure (as it did in the early 1970s in Britain) but these increases neither cause the problem nor solve it. They help maintain demand, or temporarily increase it, but do not give rise to increased output in productive industry, or change long-term plans. Conversely, monetarist policies (based on pious hopes that market forces will stimulate the productive sector) which aim to reduce public spending and to transfer resources to production, also fail. Since there are no real factors to increase demand, all that happens is that output falls. Thus monetarist measures are capable of reducing national income quite dramatically but not, in the long or the short run, of increasing it.

This stage of industrial development has only been reached in Britain at the present time. However, eventually all industrialising nations − even Japan and Liechtenstein − will reach their limits, and growth will slow down. Countries that industrialise later will tend to grow richer than those that industrialised first, but all will eventually encounter the problem of growth.

Ever since Ricardo, capitalist political economy has rested on theories of economic growth in that it claimed to show that industrialisation could make all classes of society better off. However, once the stage of absolute automation is reached, Ricardo's own analysis showed that what has become the largest class, industrial workers, must necessarily become worse off. Once output stops expanding, increased mechanisation can only take place at the expense of the incomes of workers. This is what will be considered in the next chapter.

2 Social consequences of the problem

(i) Automation and income distribution

In the first chapter I described a situation in which rapid technological change was occurring, machines were being substituted for human labour, but output was not being increased – the situation of the British economy in recent years. In deference to the author of the chapter 'On Machinery', we might refer to this as the 'Ricardo phenomenon'. In this chapter I want to analyse the long-term effects on incomes of this phenomenon.

If processes of production continue to become more and more automated without there being increases in output, fewer and fewer incomes will be distributed by productive industry, and more and more people will become dependent on the state for support. In Britain in the 1970s this trend has partly been offset by increases in services, office and administrative employment. However, new technology will increasingly affect these jobs in the 1980s, so that employment outside productive industry will also shrink. There will thus be two quite separate major sources of income for consumption – a decreasing number of people will receive wages and salaries, and an increasing number will have to claim on the state for subsistence.

Even a fully automated productive system, which required no workers at all, would 'distribute' at least the same amount of money through the sale of its output as it required through production costs. However, this income would necessarily go to those who owned or financed the machinery and not to the workers, since none would be employed. In the economy that corresponded to such a system, money would thus circulate between banks and business corporations, but none would reach the pockets of ordinary people – except through employment in the network of non-automated or semi-automated services. The latter network would give rise to some incomes for workers, but not necessarily very substantial ones.

Thus what distinguishes the stage of 'absolute automation', reached by Britain recently, from the stage of relative automation is the fact that the incomes of workers must fall as new technology is introduced. If output is the same, and automation saves labour costs, then the total incomes of the working class must decline. The 'Ricardo phenomenon' is thus a recipe for automated poverty for a growing proportion of the population – a process we in Britain have seen developing in the past decade.

The other characteristic of this stage of industrialisation is that only the state can provide incomes for consumption for this increasing sector of its citizens. In the stage of automation, the state's role in income maintenance ceases to be simply one of providing subsistence for those unable to work. It becomes one of providing for a growing number of people of working age. This causes confusion and conflict, and the polarisation of political opinion over questions of social policy, as we have seen in Britain in the 1970s.

This new role for the state is a very delicate one in a capitalist system. On the one hand, the state's function becomes one of defending the overall living standards of the working class, and protecting individuals and families from the threat of starvation. On the other hand, those workers still in employment, many of whom gain in income from automation and productivity deals, resent the increasing burden of taxation that falls on them to finance this role of the state. Furthermore, the institutions by which the state provides incomes are the ones traditionally used to regulate and control the poor, and especially to ration or punish the 'undeserving' – traditionally the able-bodied of working age. Thus claimants of state benefits do not experience the state's role as benevolent or generous, and they in turn become bitter and resentful.

Yet in the stage of absolute automation, the state alone has the power to guarantee the incomes of the working class. Productive industry no longer provides a growing amount of earnings; increasingly it cannot even support the existing population. Only the power of the state can maintain living standards, and only through the state can the working class achieve its economic and social purposes. As automation progresses, workers will become increasingly aware of this, and turn away from struggles for higher earnings at the workplace, towards more political action, focused on gaining control of the institutions of state power.

The role of the state in providing incomes for consumption cuts across the 'natural' development of capitalism, and interferes with the economic and social consequences of its development. Without this interference, the economic system would simply allow surplus population to starve. Once absolute automation becomes a long-term stage of development, the incomes of workers must continue to decline, and nothing in the productive system will remedy its social consequences. Hence the state's incomes for consumption are not part of that system. There is no logical reason why state incomes for consumption should even be in the same currency as that used to finance production. The state could issue vouchers, or meal tickets, or housing tokens; indeed this is what already happens within the social security system in the manner in which certain benefits, like free milk or lodging allowances, are distributed to certain claimants. I mention this to illustrate the separation between the process of production and income provision that would occur in a fully automated economy. Money earnings, which in economic theory are supposed to link production with consumption, would no longer effectively do so.

It is worth briefly considering what orthodox economic theory says about the distribution of incomes, to indicate the radical changes of thinking that are required to understand the stage of absolute automation.

(ii) Economic theory

Economic theory is inevitably a product of the kind of economic system in which it develops. It is a theory about how we produce goods and exchange them. The first systems for producing and exchanging goods were extremely simple. Men and women worked with their hands to make what they needed; if they needed things they could not make, they exchanged the surplus of what they made for these other goods. Historically, all theory developed from the notion of such an economy based on barter. All theory started from the notion of exchanging goods with goods, and labour with goods. With the introduction of capitalist methods of production, and money as a means of trade, the theories that developed were necessarily more complex; but ultimately they all rested on the barter system.

Thus, for the orthodox theorists of the nineteenth century, there was no problem about the distribution of incomes – or at most there were only very temporary problems. Even in the chaotic world of commerce and industry that was created by urbanisation and factory production, theory rested reassuringly on the simplicities of bartering goods. It was a fundamental law that the sum of money incomes generated by producing goods was equal to the prices of those goods, and would remain so no matter how many extra goods were produced, or by what new processes. For, as John Stuart Mill wrote,[1]

> What constitutes the means of payment for commodities is simply commodities. Each person's means of paying for the production of other people consists of those which he himself possesses. Could we suddenly double the productive power of the country, we should double the supply of commodities in every market; but we should, by the same stroke, double the purchasing power.

Yet despite the virtual unanimity of theorists about the impossibility, in principle, of producing more than could be consumed, the world of business was afflicted by a series of cyclical crises throughout the nineteenth and earlier twentieth centuries. These were serious enough to cause increased bankruptcies, higher unemployment, reduced production and falling prices. During the most spectacular of these, in the 1930s, John Maynard Keynes developed a sophisticated explanation of how aggregate demand could, after all, fall short of the aggregate supply of goods at cost-covering prices.

This analysis depended on the recognition of a more complex role for money than that allowed by classical theory, and how, in the short run, increased holdings of money could contribute to deficient aggregate demand. By deciding to save more, and to postpone consumption, individuals could, during a period of under employment of resources, add to a downward spiral of business activity. However, while rejecting the reassurance of the barter basis of economics – the certainties of the market – Keynes substituted a new form of reassurance.

He argued that government could prevent or ameliorate periodic recessions by adjustments in taxation and in public expenditure. By giving people more to spend, government could increase the capacity to consume; by spending more itself, it could contribute directly to investment as well as consumption. Thus the 'fault' which Keynes diagnosed in the market system could be remedied, and more consistent economic growth could be assured.

One feature of Keynes's theories was that the negative consequences of an increased desire to save money, rather than spend it on producing or consuming goods, only came into effect in conditions where both labour and capital were underemployed. Consequently, his theory suggested that it was greatly in the interests of government to promote full employment; and that if this could be achieved, little short of gross mismanagement of the economy could hinder economic growth. Just as Mill suggested that no increase in the power to produce goods could harm an economy, so Keynes gave no reason why the introduction of more efficient means of production should not, with government regulating aggregate demand, lead to a general increase in prosperity.

Keynesian theory is therefore about how money can be made to go on playing a satisfactory 'bridging' role between production and consumption. It recognises that something can go wrong in this process — that because of preferences in relation to money and goods, too little money can be available for consuming what is produced. But it fails to account for the 'Ricardo phenomenon'. (It is unfortunate, in fact, that Keynes reminded us of Ricardo's dismissal of Malthus's theory of under-consumption, and neglected his chapter on machinery. Thus Keynes claimed Malthus as a forerunner of modern macroeconomics, while blaming Ricardo for the relegation of aggregate demand to an economic non-issue. In retrospect, it could be argued that Ricardo provided clues to the problems of growth and income distribution which Keynes — following Malthus — obscured.)

However, Keynes was implicitly recognising a new role for the state in economic affairs, because he was showing that during the stage of advanced industrialisation the state's intervention was necessary to allow incomes to continue to rise steadily. Thus he argued what orthodox economists up to that point had always refused to recognise — that the working class was vulnerable to the processes of industrialisation, and required state action to safeguard it against unnecessary hardship. Where he was misleading was in suggesting that this was a short-run phenomenon, and a consequence of monetary factors, rather than of essential features in the development of capitalism.

Keynes failed to recognise that the vulnerability of labour lay in its role under capitalism, rather than in certain temporary economic situations. As industrialisation progressed, labour ceased to be an independent factor in production. Workers no longer owned their tools, and made products by hand. They sold their labour power to capitalists, who owned the means of production. Hence they were increasingly at risk, as industrialisation proceeded, of becoming redundant to the productive process. Once automation ceased to be relative, and started to be absolute, workers who had nothing but their labour power to sell were without means of subsistence, and depended on the state.

Thus the bartering basis of economic theory was increasingly misleading. Labour no longer produced commodities which were its own to trade in the market-place. Its earnings were dependent on machinery, which it did not own, and never could own under capitalism. Although money appeared to link production with consumption in the same direct way as in a hand-made economy, the true facts of the industrial system were very different.

As Ricardo showed in Chapter 31, money ceases to be a satisfactory bridge when capitalists choose to replace workers by machines without increasing output. If machinery is used to save labour costs, profits increase but wages and employment fall. So long as capitalists regard labour as costly, and do not anticipate increases in demand, they will continue to use any increase in profits to save more labour, by installing more automated processes. For at least ten years now, this has been the primary motivation of British productive industry. Ask any businessman how he plans his investment and production for the next ten years, and he will answer in these terms.

The experience of the Heath government showed us that Keynesian fiscal and monetary policies do not alter these attitudes. The Heath government reduced taxation, rapidly increased the money supply and greatly expanded public spending – all in an attempt to reduce unemployment (see Chapter 4). The policies failed. Unemployment remained stubbornly around the same level as it had been when the Heath government took office. Such increases in employment as did take place were not in the productive system – in spite of considerable injections of credit into private industry by government. Employment in services, office work, and above all central and local government themselves, grew rapidly under Heath's Conservatives. But firms used the extra money that these policies made available to them in furthering the processes of automation. Modest levels of growth occurred, but at a terrible price in inflation, which gobbled up most of the increases in wages. Thus Heath's government was forced to use extensions of the benefit system – and particularly the supplementation of low wages – as a means of distributing incomes for consumption, even at a time when all other Keynesian methods of increasing demand were being employed.

These failures gave Keynesian policies a terribly bad name, and revived accusations made by Keynes's opponents since the 1930s that measures based on his theory were inherently inflationary. In fact, the drastic inflation triggered off by the Heath government's measures (which continued for two years under Labour) was as much a consequence of the 'Ricardo phenomenon' as of the measures themselves. Before the 1970s, fiscal and monetary means of stimulating demand had always succeeded in boosting productive output and employment. Because of the change in business attitudes that had taken place in the late 1960s, and the acceleration of technological change, they did neither to any significant extent in the 1970s. Technological alternatives to the employment of more labour were far more attractive for businessmen, and neither long-term home demand prospects nor the world trading situation invited a prospect for expanding output. Consequently, new money made available to industry did not reach the wage packets of the working class. Instead, still more public expenditure had to be made available for increasing social security benefits, and for employing more staff in social service agencies. This was the real source of inflation.

However, monetarist economists were quick to take advantage of the failure of Keynesian measures. They made a great deal of theoretical capital out of inflation, particularly where it was combined first with low growth, and then with no growth at all (from 1974 onwards). They exploited the 'Ricardo phenomenon' to their advantage. In the United States, Milton Friedman pointed out that between 1965 and 1974 productivity (output per person) rose by 23 per cent, but real spendable weekly earnings were lower in 1974 than they had been in 1965.[2] As well as blaming reckless increases in the money supply for inflation, Friedman pointed to the huge increases in public expenditure on income support as a major factor in higher taxes on earnings. Friedman described inflation as being simultaneously a hidden tax on incomes and a means of financing the over-ambitious interventionist policies of Keynesian governments, interfering both in business affairs, and in the day-to-day lives of citizens, through their mistaken attempts to manage demand. Monetarist pressures for a return to reliance on market prices grew on both sides of the Atlantic.

In fact, the monetarists were blaming the consequences of the 'Ricardo phenomenon' for causing it. Neither in the United States nor in Britain did governments seek to extend their role of income maintenance. In both they were forced to do so by the persistence of poverty and unemployment. In Britain, this was associated with low growth; in America, with rather higher growth. But in both, because of increased automation average wages of the whole workforce were not increasing in line with productivity. High-wage employment was decreasing, and the only employment to grow was low-wage, low-productivity work, requiring state subsidisation. Governments were reluctantly dragged into the business of income support because the productive system was not distributing its increased supply of money to its workers, but was using it to substitute them by machines.

Monetarist theory has the appeal of a simple panacea. Because it shows that inflation has recently been associated both with increases in the money supply and higher public expenditure, it invites the easy conclusion that prices will steady and incomes will rise if the money supply is controlled and public expenditure is cut. Friedman insists that Keynes did not have information about the money supply in the 1920s and 1930s at his disposal when he framed his theory, or he too would have recognised that this was *the* factor which determined the level of prices. Accordingly it is market prices and not government that alone can determine the proper levels of employment and wages, and guarantee long-term growth – and hence prosperity for all.

However, the harder face of monetarism has emerged in the late 1970s, and is clearly visible in 1980. The monetarist explanation for the 'Ricardo phenomenon', in so far as it is recognised at all, is that wages are too high. According to theorists like Hayek, Keynesian policies have artificially preserved uneconomic and inefficient firms, and allowed trade unions to push wages above the level that market prices would allow. Budget deficits have been used to rescue lame ducks and finance unrealistic wage increases. The result is that productive industry's resources are maldistributed, with too many workers in outdated firms, earning wages which cannot be sustained without government support. Only massive redundancy and lower wages can ensure that these workers are redeployed in more profitable industries, and resources are freed for new firms to be established.

Attractive though these theories may be, they provide no answer to the problem posed by the 'Ricardo phenomenon'. Even if wages can be brought down by massive unemployment, and the closure of a large section of manufacturing industry (a process already well under way in 1980) this will not alter the long-term plans of those businesses that survive. Profitable firms will simply weather the storm, and then press ahead with plans for automation. The whole process will greatly add to the problem of dependence on state support. With 3 or even 5 million unemployed, the government will have to maintain a high level of public expenditure to prevent starvation. No amount of persecution of the unemployed, or cuts in benefits, can coerce employers to take on more labour while cheaper and more efficient automatic methods of production are being made available every year.

(iii) The 'Ricardo phenomenon' and social policy

Even though neither governments nor economic theorists have recognised the stage of absolute automation in Britain for what it is, they have been forced to deal with its social consequences. While promising that economic growth and higher employment can be achieved, they have had to adopt some policies to counter the fall in productive employment and the decline in the incomes of the working class.

As I showed in the first chapter, the 'Ricardo phenomenon' began to occur in the 1960s. From 1968 onwards, productivity was increasing more rapidly than incomes, and unemployment was rising. But the Wilson government and (during its first year in office) the Heath government were determined not to increase public spending to offset these trends. They wanted the modernisation of industry and the redeployment of labour to high-technology employment to occur unimpeded, and they feared balance of payments crises and inflation. Consequently, between 1968 and 1971 total public expenditure increased by only 8 per cent in real terms (in 1969 it actually fell).

However, between 1971 and 1975 total public spending increased by 30 per cent. As the Heath government saw unemployment approaching the 1 million mark, it despaired of its other attempts to encourage growth and more employment, and adopted a full-blown Keynesian approach, based mainly on increases in expenditure on social services. As I shall show in Chapter 4, this was completely contrary to its election pledges.

One major aspect of this expansion of the social services was in council house building, where spending increased by 104 per cent between 1971 and 1975. But the other main element was a very large increase in employment in the social services. Between 1971 and 1975 expenditure on wages and salaries grew by 62 per cent in education, by 53 per cent in the National Health Service, and by 101 per cent in the personal social services. This was clearly a direct response both to unemployment in the economy as a whole, and to the failure of other methods to produce any significant growth of national income. But it was also an effort to increase the 'social wage' of the working class at a time when real incomes from earnings were rising very slowly, if at all.

From 1975 onwards, the monetarist critique of these measures began to affect government policies. Total public expenditure fell, and spending on wages and salaries in the social services was cut. However, as unemployment rose to 1.5 million, spending on social security benefits increased. In the four years before 1975, this aspect of state expenditure had expanded at the fairly modest rate of 23 per cent; in the three years after 1975 it increased by the same amount, in spite of the fact that spending on all the other social services was being cut. Thus even when the Labour government was being influenced by monetarist views of public expenditure, it was forced to spend more on social security benefits simply to maintain a large sector of the population at subsistence levels.

It is widely assumed that Britain has more generous social security benefits than other countries. In reality, Britain has always devoted a lower share of national income to social security than its European neighbours, as Table 2.1 indicates.[3]

Table 2.1

	UK	Denmark	Netherlands	Italy	France	Belgium	W. Germany
Percentage of GNP spent on social security benefits in 1960	6.4	6.8	7.7	7.9	8.3	8.8	10.4

By the mid-1970s, Britain spent 7.7 per cent of GDP on income maintenance, compared with an average of 10.6 for all the EEC countries. By this time, France had expanded its income maintenance provision to 12.4 per cent of GDP, Germany also to 12.4 per cent and Italy to 10.4 per cent.[4]

The expansion in income maintenance provision that was made in

Britain during the 1970s was preponderantly in the form of means-tested selective benefits. As the 'Ricardo phenomenon's' effects were increasingly felt in the economy, the main increases were for people of working age, and took the form of supplementary benefits, rebates and supplements. None of these benefits were provided according to the principles of the Beveridge Welfare State; all represented returns to the means-tested principle of the Poor Law. Both political parties advocated improved universal benefits when in opposition, but rejected them as too expensive when in office.

Even so, as absolute automation reduced the total earnings of workers, social security benefits became a larger proportion of the incomes of the working class — in employment as well as out of work. Table 2.2 indicates the increasing importance of state income maintenance support in the weekly incomes of households.[5]

This was certainly not the intention of governments of either party. At no time did any political manifesto recognise the role of the state in guaranteeing incomes of people in work. Neither party has foreseen a growing role of government in offsetting the effects of automation. On the contrary, both have emphasised the importance of achieving growth based on new technology, and the certainty that this would produce more employment and higher wages. Thus the issue of income maintenance for people of working age has become important, as the new Conservative government attempts to cut social security benefits, while unemployment rates continue to rise.

(iv) New technology

These changes have taken place in the early stages of the 'technological revolution' based on the silicon chip. The full effects of such innovations as microprocessors and robot methods of production will not be evident for several years. However, it is already possible to recognise the new processes of automation as having potentialities for change which go far beyond earlier mechanisations. Previously, machines appeared to be ways of making each worker more productive. Lathes and welding kits could be seen as highly sophisticated versions of hand tools. Robot assemblers and robot welders are recognisable as super-productive substitute workers. An electric typewriter helps a typist be quicker and more efficient; an electronic word-processor makes her redundant.

Table 2.2

	1969	1972	1974	1976	1978
Total income (£)	32.47	42.85	58.33	82.30	106.13
Income from wages (£)	23.92	32.36	42.25	60.23	76.10
Percentage of total from wages	73.7	75.5	72.4	73.2	71.7
Incomes from social security benefits (£)	2.87	3.92	5.45	8.68	12.50
Percentage of total from social security	8.8	9.1	9.3	10.5	11.8

Microelectronics in particular threaten jobs because they will revolutionise the kind of employment that has been increasing, even as the productive workforce has been shrinking. Administrative, technical and clerical workers as a percentage of all workers employed in manufacturing industry increased from 22.8 per cent in 1964 to 27.6 per cent in 1977. Outside manufacturing industry, the growth has been much more rapid; for example, employment in financial, professional and scientific services increased from 3,170,000 in 1964 to 4,709,000 in 1978. All these jobs are to some extent threatened by new technology in the processing, storing and utilisation of information based on the word-processor and electronic communication within and between offices. The cost-effectiveness of the new technology is already clear. The head of research of a white-collar trade union was recently quoted as saying,[6]

A typist in Central London probably costs £6,000 to £7,000 per annum in salary, employment costs, social insurance, etc., for an employer, and the evidence which I have seen indicates that if you use it properly, you can replace a typist by installing a word-processor which costs £4,000; then you can save the cost of a word-processor in twelve months.

For the first time, it is suddenly possible to imagine a world in which machines have taken over almost all of the work previously done by people — something unimaginable before the new technology was developed. The notion of a totally automated system of production and distribution — all goods being made by robots, programmed by computers, which in time guide remote-controlled vehicles to distribute them to 'shops' where other computers dispense them — is no longer pure science fiction. If such a notion seems remote, it is suddenly no less remote than the world of the craftsman, using only hand tools, and bartering his products — the world reflected by economic theory. Production does not obey the laws of economics — it makes them. New theories are required to understand the stage of absolute auto-mation.

In the first chapter, I argued that the Ricardian theory of economic growth assumed the existence of a low-productivity agricultural sector and a growing population, which would provide an ever-larger indus-trial workforce to expand manufacturing production. Yet if the whole process of technological change is a transition from an entirely hand-made to an entirely machine-made economy, then the manufacturing workforce cannot continue to grow indefinitely. I suggested that in Britain the point had already been reached in the 1960s when workers were being replaced by machines in the productive sector of the economy; in the 1980s this process will begin in the non-productive sector, through microelectronics.

A fully automated world would provide much less work for workers to do, and far fewer incomes in the form of wages and salaries. If some other more equitable way of providing income for consumption could be introduced, this could be a highly desirable future, allowing every-one the leisure to cultivate human relationships and cultural activities, leaving to machines the whole business of pursuing commercial and industrial activities and goals. However, the only means of ensuring that this occurred would be for the power of the state to be used against the dominant economic order. So long as governments try to harness the development of the economy to provide higher earnings, absolute automation will simply continue to reduce incomes.

Since the mid-1960s, social policy under both parties has been derived entirely from plans for economic growth. Promises of increased social provision have rested on targets for expanding the economy which have proved quite illusory. In addition to failures of growth, Britain has experienced unexpectedly high levels of unemployment and poverty, which in turn have required relief. Short-term expe-dients have been adopted to deal with these problems, but, with con-tinued failure to expand, these have become structural features of the welfare system. The clearest example of this is supplementary benefits. Originally the scheme was intended to replace National Assistance, which in turn had been planned by Beveridge as a small, residual and diminishing service for the few who fell below the level of National

Insurance benefits. Supplementary benefits were supposed to reduce stigma and establish minimal rights to assistance, but not to become a massive feature of the income maintenance system. In fact, by 1978 their role had grown so much that they were deemed to be in need of reform, to make them 'simpler and fairer' and adapt them to their

Table 2.3

Numbers on supplementary benefits and allowances (thousands)	1968	1969	1970	1971	1972	1973	1974	1975	1976	1977
Unemployed	220	228	239	387	392	249	301	541	654	703
Single parents (other than widows)	157	177	191	213	227	228	245	276	303	323

'mass role'. The fact that the large increase in claimants of supplementary benefits was concentrated among those of working age is shown by the figures given in Table 2.3.[7] By 1976 there were 1,181,000 dependent children in families living on supplementary benefits.

Supplementary benefits are a prime example of a means-tested benefit whose conditions for eligibility restrict the freedom and dignity of the recipient. Claimants are not merely constrained as to what they and other members of their family may own or earn; they are also limited by regulations as to what they may do, where they may live, and with whom; and they are subject to official discretion as to whether they are deemed eligible at all. The rate of benefits is intentionally kept at a subsistence level, and the stigma attached to claiming is reflected in media labels such as 'scroungers' and 'layabouts'. It is no coincidence that as numbers on supplementary benefits have increased, prejudice against welfare beneficiaries generally has magnified.

Selective methods of relieving poverty and unemployment have deepened the divisions between workers and claimants. Those who still earn sufficient to remain 'independent' of state support resent what they perceive as the burden of welfare dependency represented by claimants. Those excluded from receiving an income from work feel shame and confusion, and are often bitter against those they see as more fortunate than themselves. Few organisations bridge the gap between the two groups; state agencies usually widen it by the stigma they confer. Mutual hostility and prejudice are constantly reinforced.

Predominantly under Labour governments, this process developed in a largely unplanned, drifting manner between 1965 and 1979. However, the new Conservative government has committed itself to economic and social policies which are much more abrasive. It links lack of growth and high unemployment with increased public spending, and claims that Britain will have to accept even higher levels of unemployment before growth can be achieved. However, it is intent on cutting state expenditure, and this includes reducing various National Insurance benefits, thus forcing an even higher proportion of claimants on to supplementary benefits and other means-tested systems. Both the extent of the social problem associated with economic failure, and the divisiveness of social policy, will be increased by Conservative measures. If the analysis of my first chapter is accepted, these results will be cumulative, and not short term as is claimed.

Finally, under both Labour and the new Conservatives there has recently been a far heavier emphasis on social control. Fears of a breakdown in law and order have grown, and welfare beneficiaries are particularly suspected of being deviant and dangerous. In the early 1970s, the personal social services were greatly expanded (real expenditure doubled in four years) and given a far more controlling role (see Chapter 8). Under the Conservatives, the police and prison services are being reinforced, and more direct threats against deviant members of the 'lower orders' are being used.

It is therefore clear that the social policies associated with technological unemployment in the past fifteen years have been far from benevolent. Instead of ushering in a golden age of leisure and human communication, new technology has created an atmosphere of social conflict, suspicion and hostility. Such leisure as has been created has been seen not as a bonus and a boon, but as a threat; the unemployed see it as enforced idleness, and the employed see it as evidence of moral depravity. Instead of being counted as a premium on productivity, increased leisure (redefined, through productivity deals, as redundancy) has been treated as a kind of tax on the hard work of those still in employment. Increasingly punitive attitudes towards the unemployed are being translated by the Conservatives into government policies, in an attempt to create a 'proper differential' between the living standards of those in work and those out of it. Technology has thus sharpened social divisions and political conflicts.

From all this it is clear that the foreseeable future will not take the form of an automated Utopia of freedom and leisure, but rather of a

deeply divided and restricted society. Present trends suggest a continued growth in the wealth and power of large business corporations
and financial institutions which own and control the means of production. Monetarist policies, accompanied by high rates of interest, will
drive smaller firms to the wall, while the only sector of the economy
to enjoy a rosy prospect in 1980 is the financial one. Even if a non-
interventionist government abdicates any attempt to regulate these
organisations, it will increasingly be drawn into the business of regulating the rest of the population.

As automation proceeds, the divisions in society will deepen along
the following lines. First, there will be a diminishing number of high-
paid workers in technologically advanced employment, encouraged to
define themselves as the life-blood of the nation, and to resent and
despise the others as inferior and dependent. Second, there will be
low-paid workers in low-technology industries and services. These will
require state subsidisation of their wages in order to achieve a subsistence income. They will have much lower status than the first group,
and a degree of coercion will be required to make them take these jobs,
as they will be little better off than the third group, and have only
slightly less stigma. Finally, there will be those who are wholly dependent on state benefits, who will be the object of the greatest official
suspicion and control, but will increasingly emerge as the largest group.
This group may be subdivided between the 'deserving' (the elderly,
disabled, sick and handicapped) and the 'undeserving' (able-bodied,
of working age and their children) — the latter being singled out for
particularly harsh treatment.

There will of course necessarily be a large number of state officials
employed to regulate the two most numerous groups in such an
economy. What are now called the social services are increasingly
emerging as agencies of social control, rationing and disciplining the
poor according to official prescriptions. The average incomes of
employees in these services are kept just above those of their clients,
a policy which creates divisions and resentment on both sides of the
official barrier.

(v) Conclusions

In the mid-1960s, government tried to harness technological change
to produce a faster rate of economic growth. In fact, new technology

led to higher rates of productivity, but not to higher output – hence the workforce shrank. In terms of growth, therefore, new technology has been neutral. In terms of full employment, it has been working against government policy, to the point where the Conservatives have abandoned full employment as a policy aim.

I have suggested that the social consequences of these developments will be a dangerous division between the employed and the non-employed, which must deepen as new technology constantly reinforces present trends. The Labour Party has repeatedly shown its inability to grasp these issues and use state power to protect the living standards of those who have suffered from the consequences of the 'Ricardo phenomenon'.

If the Labour Party had been able to predict in 1964 that the economy would not grow at anything like the target rate it set, and that the productive workforce would shrink in the long term, it would have been in a dilemma. As a party trying to establish a new consensus at the centre of British politics that would make it the new natural party of government, Labour was bidding to outdo the Conservatives in its claims for promoting industrial efficiency and expansion. Social policy played a second fiddle: better social services were seen as a by-product of faster growth, and even then Labour's priorities gave social services a far smaller share of the cake than they had in Britain's European neighbours (see Chapter 6). If Labour had believed that the economy would not and could not grow, it would have had to decide whether to adopt long-term measures with explicitly repressive implications for the poor, or to try to create a more free and equal society.

As it was, Labour was able to use the aspirations of the middle classes, and the better-off working class, to gain support for its plans for technologically based growth and higher productivity, promising always that the expansion this would one day provide would give full employment and better social services. Its social policies, though expedient and short-sighted, were never sufficiently abrasive to antagonise the working class, even though their results were highly oppressive for claimants. It was not until the new Conservative government took office that the full implications of social policies adopted under Labour began to be made clear. As trade unions and the labour movement become aware of these implications, there are at last signs that the working class will unite with claimants in resisting the consequences of absolute automation.

In this process, social policy options which had long been discarded will again come up for consideration. Work-sharing will be taken seriously as an alternative to productivity-dealing and redundancy. Higher universal benefits will be pressed for as more equitable than an extension of the means test. Increased child benefits will be urged, and a guaranteed maintenance allowance for single parents (recommended by the Finer Report in 1974, but ignored by the Labour government) will again be put on the agenda for social reform. It will be argued that all these measures would produce a more just and less divided society, and would give far less fuel to Conservative criticisms of the Welfare State, and workers' resentments of its beneficiaries.

However, it has taken a recession, reinforced by an aggressively monetarist government, and a vast increase in unemployment, to begin this change of heart. Both the Labour Party and the trade union leadership have based all their policies for the past fifteen years on exaggerated hopes of growth. They have supported productivity-dealing and redundancies in the expectation that workers would be redeployed to more productive and efficient industries, and output would rise. These attitudes will not change quickly. The Labour Party and trade union leaderships will cling to power, and to policies which they regard as necessary to attract a middle ground of basically materialistic and self-interested voters, who are more interested in general prosperity than in the plight of minority disadvantaged groups. It is only as this minority becomes significant, and then within sight of becoming a majority, that the tide will turn against them. I would predict that it will only be after Labour (as a result of its internal strife) loses the election of 1984, despite unemployment of over 3 million, that the long knives will be out, and the pragmatic managerial politics of the past fifteen years may be replaced by policies that are truly socialist.

This will not happen until the rank and file of ordinary workers recognise the implications of new technology. Microelectronics and robot methods of production will not give us great economic growth in Britain, for all the reasons given in the first chapter. They could give us a much more leisurely, pleasant and human life-style. Productivity deals could be based on an expectation not of higher earnings but of more leisure. Bargains could be made for shorter hours, rather than for higher wages and redundancies.

Alternatively, where new processes do not permit this, policies could be aimed at increasing universal benefits in line with increased productivity. Thus state assistance *for all* (in the form of measures like child benefits, paid to workers and claimants alike, and other non-means tested income supplements) could be developed as incomes from wages diminish — as they surely must. Instead of providing a stigmatised subsistence for those condemned to enforced idleness under suspicious surveillance, the state could start to provide a guaranteed minimum income for all. Increased benefits for everyone, including those of working age, are the only realistic policy in view of the eventual mechanisation of all productive and much non-productive work. State income maintenance should, in a fully automated economy, be the main source of consumption, and not a subsidiary one. But only a total rejection of past attitudes and policies could bring into existence a society in which new technology increased social welfare and cohesion, rather than causing division and conflict.

In Part 2 of this book I shall trace the history of economic policy in Britain, and show how Keynesian and monetarist measures alike have failed to solve the problem of economic growth. In Part 3 I shall show how social policies reacted to these failures, and how the state came increasingly to rely on social control. In the final chapters I shall consider political alternatives, and look at the policies necessary to reconcile automation with socialist principles.

Part 2

3 Economic policy 1964-70

(i) The onset of the 'Ricardo phenomenon'

In the first chapter I argued that the origins of the 'Ricardo phenomenon' in Britain could be traced to the mid-1960s, when productive employment started to decline, but productivity continued to increase. In this chapter I shall look in more detail at this period, and consider how the Labour government's economic policies influenced this process.

It is now generally accepted by economists that this period was a crucial turning-point in the post-war economic development of Britain. The Labour government was committed to a plan for improving the rate of growth of the economy, giving highest priority to industrial expansion. Yet it is to this same government's term of office that the problem of 'too few producers' — now widely accepted as the diagnosis of our economic ills — can be traced. Once again I shall consider Bacon and Eltis's analysis of the origins of this problem, and show how it differs from my own.

They argue that this was an era of lost opportunities because[1]

Britain could have achieved almost everything for which the most optimistic hoped . . . . in Britain from 1962 onwards output per man-hour in manufacturing industry started to advance at an annual rate of 4.2 per cent in place of the mere 2.2 per cent per annum achieved from 1951 to 1962. . . . If this greatly increased potential had been turned into faster actual growth, as it could and should have been, Britain would have had about one-and-a-half times as much growth from 1962 onwards as it achieved up to then. The higher growth rate in Mr. George Brown's *National Plan* of 1965, 3.8 per cent per

annum, required almost exactly the rate of growth of labour productivity in industry, 4.1 per cent per annum, that was actually
achieved throughout the period 1962-1975 . . . . so far as productivity
was concerned, and this is the crucial factor that determines the
potential growth rate of an economy, Mr. George Brown's plan was
spot on.

What then was the source of Britain's failure to take this chance?
Bacon and Eltis suggest that we needed literally to capitalise on the
opportunity. To achieve the targets set for growth, industrial investment needed to be increased much more rapidly than before 1962.
Investment in industry needed to rise from a proportion of 7.2 per
cent of industrial production in 1962 to something like 12 per cent to
take full advantage of the chance for growth. In fact it did increase,
both under the Conservatives and under Labour, and by 1966 stood
at 8.8 per cent of industrial production. According to Bacon and
Eltis this was 'exactly what was needed',[2] to be on target for the
planned increase in the rate of growth of the economy. Yet that same
year the whole plan was scrapped.

Thus the crucial question is why the Labour government abandoned
its targets for growth in 1966, and adopted the standard deflationary
measures of the previous decade just when these targets were, according
to Bacon and Eltis, within its scope to achieve. Bacon and Eltis devote
only a couple of paragraphs to this question in their book, and their
explanation is highly implausible. They suggest that government over-
estimated the balance of payments deficit, and wrongly rejected devaluation of the pound as a possible solution to this problem. It hastily
cut expenditure on investment in the public sector, and withdrew its
commitment to growth. This let private industry down, because
'businessmen . . . had co-operated with the Plan by investing ahead of
demand.'[3] As a result, they began to lay off workers in their sector of
productive industry. This started a decline in productive employment
that has continued ever since.

As I shall show, this whole analysis does not hold together theo-
retically, nor does it explain the facts of what happened. At a theoretical level, Bacon and Eltis have treated productivity as determined
by technological change. They therefore take the rate of increase in
productivity as a constant factor in their model — as providing the
potential for growth, the dynamic of which comes from industrial
investment. Their argument implies that higher investment in industry

would necessarily have produced higher output. Yet as I showed in Chapter 1, with rapid technological change investment can be used either for increasing output or for saving long-term labour costs. Before 1966, increased investment was already failing to produce the expansion in output that the government needed in order to achieve its targets. The abandonment of the National Plan was as much a result of this failure as of balance of payments problems − which in any case were related to it.

Second, even though industrial investment in the public sector was severely cut back in 1966, investment in the private sector continued to rise. In other words, businessmen's investment decisions were not much influenced by the change in the government's plans. Both before and after 1966, private industry was using new technology mainly to save labour costs, and not to expand output. The change that took place in 1966 was in the public sector, where because of the failure of private industry to increase production, both investment and output were cut back.

To trace the onset of the 'Ricardo phenomenon' we need to consider what the government was trying to achieve, and what setbacks it encountered.

(ii) The Wilson programme

Labour's election victory in 1964 provides a convenient starting-point for the analysis, because Labour's programme was designed precisely to increase growth through new technology. The election manifesto was broadly followed in the National Plan of 1965, which set targets for growth, investment and productivity.

The manifesto contained three main elements:

(a) An emphasis on the importance of planning as a means to greater efficiency and faster economic growth.
(b) A strategy for modernisation of industry, based on increased investment, and greater use of new technology.
(c) An attempt to improve productivity, arising from modernisation, but also involving a reduction of restrictive practices, and the redeployment and retraining of manpower.

(a) Planning

The notion of economic planning was part of the Labour Party's heritage from the 1945-51 government. However, Harold Wilson sought to rid it of its overtones of rationing and restriction, and to present planning as a necessary means to injecting a new dynamism into the economy. The longest section of the party election manifesto — 'Planning the New Britain' — dealt with the need to mobilise the whole country behind a national plan for expansion, towards targets which 'will only be achieved by Socialist planning.'[4]

The Conservative government had been converted to some sort of planning (roughly patterned on the French model) in 1961. Spurred on by a group of industrialists and economists who wanted faster expansion, they had set up the National Economic Development Council (NEDC) in 1962. The aim was to achieve a more even and sustained rate of growth — in face of mounting criticisms of their 'stop-go' policies of the previous ten years. In their attempt to stave off recurrent balance of payments crises, government had alternated between sudden bursts of inflation and deflation of demand, which reinforced rather than offset the cyclical fluctuations of the economy. The NEDC had produced a rather tentative plan for a 4 per cent growth rate, and set targets for investment, imports and exports needed to achieve this rate of expansion. In 1964 the target rate for imports was greatly exceeded, but Bacon and Eltis argue that a Conservative government might well have continued to succeed in financing an increase in industrial investment out of a balance of payments deficit if the Conservatives had won the election. A Labour government was much more vulnerable to foreign scepticism about its policies, and therefore had to adopt more orthodox strategies to implement its plans.

Accordingly, the Wilson government committed itself to a defence of the pound and ruled out devaluation within a few days of taking office. Many commentators later identified this as the fatal step that undermined Labour's plans for expansion. The new government was constantly aware of the need to restrict demand in order to control imports, and was therefore limited in its commitment to growth. None the less, it remained convinced of the need for planning, and set up more elaborate administrative machinery for its implementation. Furthermore, unlike its NEDC predecessor, the Labour plan was aimed specifically at modernisation and higher productivity.

(b) Modernisation of industry

Both before and after the election victory, Labour's leaders emphasised the modernisation of industry as the primary aim of its programme. The manifesto announced that a new Ministry of Economic Affairs would 'frame the broad strategy for increasing investment, expanding exports and replacing inessential imports.' It would be a plan to 're-vitalise and modernise the whole economy,' based on 'injecting modern technology into our industries'.[5]

In a television broadcast on 24 February 1965, Harold Wilson took up the same theme.[6]

This has to be a total national effort. This is first and foremost a job of production: producing more and producing cheaply. It means harnessing to our peacetime job, as we did in wartime, all the re-sources of skill and science and technology; ruthlessly modernising our traditional industries, no matter who gets hurt; purposefully expanding the new challenging industries, which, here and else-where, are being created on the frontiers of science.

In addition to creating the Department of Economic Affairs, the new government set up a Ministry of Technology, 'to guide and stimu-late a major national effort to bring advanced technology and new pro-cesses into industry'.[7] Speaking to the Economic Club of New York on 14 April 1965, the Prime Minister claimed that the ministry was attack-ing the problems of[8]

the new growth industries where not long ago Britain was in the forefront of progress and where we have fallen behind. I am thinking here of computers and of electronics. For the first time in our history the problems of these industries have been tackled on a nation-wide basis with state power and even state finance to speed the application of these techniques throughout industry and to modernise our production side.

In the last years of the Conservative government, the NEDC had tried to improve the rate of investment in industry. Industrial invest-ment rose by only 1 per cent between 1962 and 1963, but it rose by 14 per cent between 1963 and 1964, and a further 6.5 per cent between 1964 and 1965. Under the Conservatives, the great bulk of the increase in investment was in the public sector. Labour's achievement was that *manufacturing* investment expanded by 25 per cent in its first two years of office.[9] This should have provided exactly the modernisation programme that was necessary for faster growth, based on increased output of manufactured goods in the private sector.

However, output did not grow as planned between 1964 and 1966, in spite of this rapid rise in industrial investment. On the contrary, output of production industries had grown by 8.3 per cent between 1963 and 1964, when industrial investment was still low, but grew by only 3.4 per cent between 1964 and 1965, and 1.5 per cent between 1965 and 1966. The figures set out in Table 3.1 illustrate the slow rate

Table 3.1

	1963	1964	1965	1966
Index of GDP (at 1963 prices)	100	105.9	108.8	110.7
Index of output of production industries (at 1963 prices)	100	108.3	111.7	113.2
Index of output of manufacturing industries (at 1963 prices)	100	108.7	112.4	114.2

of growth of the economy as a whole after 1964 and particularly of productive industry and the manufacturing sector of it, in spite of the expansion of investment.[10] The real source of the Labour government's difficulties was this slow response of industrial output to increased investment.

(c) Productivity and manpower

The third main strand of Labour's programme did not feature largely in the party's election manifesto, but became a dominant theme of the Prime Minister's post-election speeches, and played a much more important part in the National Plan of 1965 than it had in the NEDC forecasts of 1962.

Doubtless one of the reasons why productivity was not mentioned in the manifesto was the possible resistance to the notion by trade unions. But speaking to the TUC in September, just before the election, Harold Wilson suggested that every major union should have its own productivity department, as a means to achieving higher wages. He pointed out that some American unions had productivity experts, who urged their members to adopt new methods to raise production and earnings. He reiterated this point in his television broadcast of 24 February 1965, and made increases in productivity a major target of the government's plans.

Meanwhile, the Department of Economic Affairs, under George Brown, succeeded, in December 1964, in persuading the employers and the trade unions to sign a joint statement of intent on productivity, prices and incomes. They agreed that[11]

major objectives of national policy must be:

— to ensure that British industry is dynamic and that its prices are competitive;
— to raise productivity and efficiency so that real national output can increase, and to keep increases in wages, salaries and other forms of incomes in line with this increase;
— to keep the general level of prices stable.

They further agreed on behalf of their members:

to encourage and lead a sustained attack on the obstacles to efficiency, whether on the part of management or of workers, and to strive for the adoption of more rigorous standards of performance at all levels.

When the National Plan was published in September 1965, it set a target of 3.4 per cent per year for improvements in productivity. This did not seem unduly optimistic, as there had been some reasonable increases in productivity between 1963 and 1965, particularly in production industries, as can be seen from Table 3.2. However, in the year following the Plan, the rate of improvement declined; it rose again slightly in the year after the Plan was abandoned.[12] Thus, in spite of the work of the new ministries and the NEDC, and in spite of agreement in principle to modernisation and productivity by both sides of industry, results in this sphere were at first rather discouraging.

The other side of Labour's programme for increasing output by

Table 3.2

	1963	1964	1965	1966	1967
Index of productivity in whole economy (GDP per head at 1963 prices)	100.0	104.5	106.5	108.1	111.4
Index of productivity in production industries (output per person employed, at 1963 prices)	100.0	106.5	108.7	110.4	114.1

means of new technology was that manpower would have to be re-deployed from older, less efficient industries to modern, more productive ones. Thus the election manifesto had a section on 'Mobility and Training', and the new government set up retraining courses and widened the scope of redundancy payments to encourage redeployment. The National Plan estimated that, for growth targets to be reached, the economy would require about 800,000 more workers by 1970, while population statistics suggested that the workforce would increase by only 400,000. Even allowing for the redeployment of 200,000 workers, this left a shortfall of about 200,000, and the Plan was widely criticised for this gap.

In the event, of course, unemployment increased throughout the period covered by the Plan, and the employed workforce, particularly in production industries, shrank (see Table 3.3). Furthermore, a trend was already evident at this early stage (though no commentator appears to have drawn attention to it) that increases in productivity varied inversely with increases in employment in productive industry. Increases in productivity were slow from 1964 to 1966, when employ-

Table 3.3

	1965	1966	1967	1968	1969	1970
Unemployed (thousands)	299	281	503	542	518	555
Workforce in production industries (thousands)	11,775	11,852	11,456	11,254	10,661	10,482
Total workforce in employment (thousands)	23,621	23,784	23,305	23,125	23,085	22,479

ment in productive industry was expanding, and speeded up dramatically from 1967, when employment was declining, eventually almost reaching the targets of the 1965 Plan. This will be discussed more fully in subsequent sections.

(iii) The failure of the National Plan of 1965

In July 1966, soon after the Labour government had been re-elected, a crisis over sterling and the balance of payments led to cuts in public expenditure, and particularly in investment in the public sector. This caused a major storm in the Cabinet, and George Brown offered to resign, seeing it as the signal that the National Plan had been scrapped. The rest of the Cabinet was apparently taken by surprise by the severity of the measures. Richard Crossman commented in his diary,[13]

> It is now pretty clear that ever since we won the election this could have happened to the pound. Yet no contingency plan of any kind has been prepared and our big three [Wilson, Brown, Callaghan] were caught completely unawares when the pound suddenly became unstuck.

This is important in understanding why the National Plan was abandoned at this point. One school of economic thought has suggested that the failure of the Plan was virtually inevitable from the moment when the new Labour government decided to give priority to the protection of the pound – immediately after it took office. The economists whose arguments for 'growth through planning' had inspired the Labour programme had tended to assume that devaluation of the pound would be necessary. In retrospect they considered that they had not made this sufficiently explicit, and argued that without it the targets of the 1965 Plan were unrealistic – particularly those for exports and imports. The economist Sam Brittan wrote in 1967,[14]

> Those who challenged the sterling-first doctrines and put forward the claims of expansion have no reason to be repentant – not even about the goal of a 4 per cent growth rate. But they should have concentrated on policies for making such a growth rate possible . . . instead of getting involved in the diversions of the planning exercises.

Yet the government's caution about the balance of payments should have made it especially aware of the possibilities of a crisis such as took place in July 1966. Therefore this view does not explain the consternation in the Cabinet about the sudden onset of the crisis, and the unexpectedness of the public expenditure cuts. It seems that the government considered that the economy was roughly on target until the summer of 1966, and was surprised by the rapid increase in imports, and the failure of exports to grow.

This leads to the second view of the crisis — Bacon and Eltis's suggestion that the government over-reacted, and unnecessarily threw away the potential for growth which abundantly existed at the time. They argue that the underlying trend in the balance of payments was favourable — that net exports had increased as a share of industrial production from 12.4 to 12.8 per cent between 1964 and 1966. But this takes no account of the government's real reason for anxiety — given its determination not to devalue — in the growth of the gap between imports and exports during the second quarter of 1966. Because Bacon and Eltis concentrate on analysing the proportions of national output going to various forms of expenditure, they do not show the failure of the economy as a whole, and the productive sector in particular, to expand its output as planned during this period. Because production did not grow, any increase in aggregate demand sucked in more imports, increasingly of manufactured goods as well as raw materials. Thus the government was constantly restraining demand — in 1964 and 1965, as well as in the first half of 1966 — and finally had to take drastic measures that amounted to a 'stop', in the traditions of its Conservative predecessors. It was this that finally caused the National Plan to be scrapped.

(iv) Consequences of the failure of the Plan

Bacon and Eltis suggest that the main effect of the abandonment of the Plan was on investment, and that this in turn led output to be unnecessarily restricted, and workers to be laid off. According to them, industrialists who had been participating enthusiastically in the government's plans for growth were suddenly left in the lurch by its change of course, and were forced to alter their plans for increasing both investment and output.

A look at the figures for these items shows that their analysis is wrong. Investment in the private sector (see Table 3.4) continued to grow after 1966, and output in productive industry, and the manufacturing sector, which was already slowing down in 1965-6, accelerated quite significantly in 1967-8 (see Table 3.5).

Table 3.4 Gross domestic fixed capital formation at 1963 prices by broad sector and type of asset[15]

Private sector	1964	1965	1966	1967	1968	1969	1970
Plant and machinery (£m.)	1,283	1,397	1,455	1,464	1,551	1,700	1,834
Other new building and works, etc. (£m.)	887	921	873	854	935	1,005	1,004

Table 3.5 Index of output at 1963 prices

	1964	1965	1966	1967	1968	1969	1970
Production industries[16]	108.3	111.7	113.2	113.9	119.8	122.9	124.2
Manufacturing industries[17]	108.7	112.4	114.2	113.2	121.4	125.6	127.2

It was in the public sector that cuts in investment plans took place, as is shown in Table 3.6. However, even though these were considerable, the growth rate of the economy as a whole was not much affected by the scrapping of the Plan. Growth was disappointing between 1964 and 1967, and much more rapid in 1967-8 (see Table 3.7). This was the period when the government had no plan for growth. In 1969 it published a more modest 'planning document' — 'The Task Ahead' — which was widely received as more realistic than its predecessor, and suggested that a pessimistic forecast would allow a growth rate of

Table 3.6 Gross domestic fixed capital formation at 1963 prices by broad sector and type of asset[18]

Public corporations	1964	1965	1966	1967	1968	1969	1970
Plant and machinery (£m.)	747	789	883	964	857	757	754
Other new buildings and works, etc. (£m.)	258	281	302	360	344	314	277

Table 3.7 Index of Gross Domestic Product at 1963 prices

1964	1965	1966	1967	1968	1969	1970
105.9	108.8	110.7	112.5	117.0	119.5	121.8

of slightly less than 3 per cent. The rate immediately fell back to about 2 per cent. However, although the failure of the Plan did not affect the overall performance of the economy significantly, it did alter the direction of economic policy under the Labour government.

The main effect of the failure of the Plan was the change from a positive policy aimed at expansion to a restrictive one, built around the control of prices and incomes. The Department of Economic Affairs was run down, and finally wound up in 1969. The Minister of Technology, Frank Cousins, resigned during the crisis of July 1966, and his ministry was merged with the Board of Trade to form the Department of Trade and Industry in 1970.

The measures of 1966 outlawed any increases in prices or wages for one year, and proved quite effective. However, the subsequent stages of the government's prices and incomes policy provoked increasing opposition from trade unions. To a large extent this stemmed from frustration with the government's failure to promote growth. After the devaluation of 1967, the TUC began to press harder for a resumption of expansionist planning; it also became increasingly critical of rising unemployment.[19]

There is a danger at the present time that Britain's potential for economic growth may once again be under-estimated. . . . Far too many men and women have found themselves without jobs in the past twelve months. Higher productivity has been achieved but the new jobs promised as part of the programme for redeployment are not yet there. . . . If the new approach to productivity proves, in the eyes of the workpeople, to have been at their expense, there will only be an inevitable tendency for them to protect themselves in the only way they know how — by restricting output and productivity and by sharing work. This would be a tragedy. . . . There is no reason why, after an initial period of adjustment, the G.D.P. should not be expanding rapidly. The rate of expansion can be put at 6 per cent in the year from mid-1968 to mid-1969. Of this total, in broad terms 4 per cent will come from an increase in hourly productivity, 1 per cent from extra hours per man and 1 per cent from increased employment.

When figures for productivity during this period are considered, the TUC's criticisms of government policy are seen to be very relevant. During this period of very low growth, productivity improved rapidly

Table 3.8

(1963 = 100)	*1966*	*1967*	*1968*	*1969*	*1970*	*1971*
Index of output (GDP, all industries and services)	110.7	112.5	117.0	119.5	121.8	123.9
Index of productivity (GDP per head, all industries and services)	108.1	111.4	116.7	119.4	122.5	126.8
Index of output (production industries)	113.2	113.9	119.8	122.9	124.2	125.0
Index of productivity (production industries)	110.4	114.1	121.7	124.9	128.2	.133.7

especially in production industries (see Table 3.8). It can be recognised that productivity started to increase more rapidly than output in the economy as a whole in 1967, and in productive industry in 1966, while the largest improvements in productivity generally occurred from 1968 onwards, when the rate of expansion was slowing down.

Table 3.9

	1966	*1967*	*1968*	*1969*	*1970*	*1971*
Unemployed (thousands)	281	503	542	518	555	724

Furthermore, during this period, unemployment was growing (see Table 3.9). The correlation between high productivity and a shrinking work-force can be seen most vividly in the figures for two industries during this period (see Table 3.10). Both mining and quarrying and textiles were among the most successful in improving productivity; they were also among the industries with the highest reductions of employees.[20]

Commenting on this trend some years later, the French economist Jacques Leruez pointed out that these improvements in productivity could not be attributed to economic changes following devaluation:[21]

what is most striking is that the increase in productivity only really begins to accelerate in 1968, while – apart from 1968 itself – the rate of expansion was beginning to slow down. Thus increases in productivity were due less to improvements in the terms of trade than to other factors, such as the influence of the Selective Employment Tax in the service sector, and probably also to productivity agreements in industry. But another factor was probably crucial: the change in the nature of investments, with new plant and machinery being designed less to increase output than to economise on manpower, as a reaction to higher labour costs.

There thus began to be a highly paradoxical chain of economic phenomena, largely promoted by government policy. The second and third stages of the prices and incomes policy increasingly urged trade unions to use productivity deals as means to higher wage bargains. Unions that took this advice increasingly found that they were bargaining away jobs; productivity-dealing included a substantial element of redundancy. Yet increases in output were small. Angered by the failure of the government to produce growth, and by higher taxation, unions increasingly pressed for higher wage settlements – the average percentage rise in the last quarter of 1969 was 7.8 (more than twice the official norm), and the rate of increase in 1970 was still higher.

Table 3.10

	1964	1966	1970	1971
Mining and quarrying				
Index of productivity (output per head, 1963 = 100)	103.3	106.5	128.8	135.5
Workforce (thousands)	661	578	407	396
Textiles				
Index of productivity (output per head, 1963 = 100)	104.0	111.7	145.1	156.8
Workforce (thousands)	840	810	678	622

Yet the real value of these increases in wages was considerably lower than it appeared. Turner and Wilkinson showed that when allowance was made for increases in taxation and National Insurance contributions, the increase in real incomes during the period was very small. For the average wage-earner with two children, it was only about 1 per cent per year between 1964 and 1968, and rose to only about 2.7 per cent in 1968-70. This compared with an annual average increase in real income of 1.9 per cent for the same wage-earner in the period 1959-64.[22]

Furthermore, the effects of productivity-based wage increases were shown in the decline in the share of national product of the bottom 50 per cent of personal incomes. Between 1964 and 1966 the share of this group increased from just over 25 per cent to just under 27 per

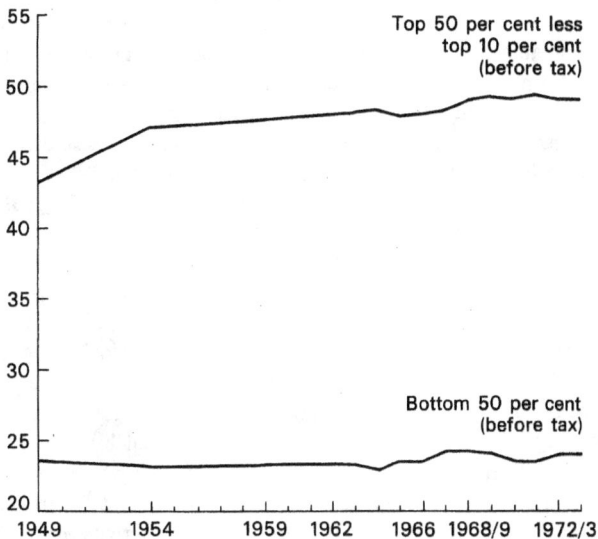

Figure 3.1 Distribution of incomes: income shares of selected quantile groups

cent before tax. By 1971 it had fallen back to 26 per cent. The share of the top 50 per cent (less the top 10 per cent) increased from 49 per cent to over 50 per cent in the period 1964-71. This is shown in Figure 3.1.[23]

Thus in this period there can be observed the beginning of some of the divisions among workers that were a feature of the 1970s. The money wages of higher-wage earners, mainly in high-productivity employment, rose fairly quickly, but this increase was offset by higher taxation, partly to finance the relief of poverty and unemployment. This was resented. Trade unionists were demanding some reward for the sacrifices made in reducing the workforce and increasing productivity. But, as was to happen with more frequency in the 1970s, they were demanding that the price for productivity deals should be paid to those workers who were retained, rather than (through higher taxation) to those made redundant. Because output was not rising fast enough, this could not be achieved without inflation.

Another source of higher government expenditure − leading to higher taxation − was the effort to modernise industry. The Industrial Reorganisation Corporation (IRC) was set up in 1966 to put money into companies with a view to modernisation. It promoted and encouraged a number of mergers between companies aimed at permitting economies of scale. Under the Industrial Expansion Act of 1968, the Ministry of Technology was also empowered to assist companies seeking to introduce new techniques or new products. Taken together with the Monopolies Commission and the Industrial Training Boards and training centres, all this constituted considerable state intervention in industry − costing an estimated £2,000 million a year by 1970. Yet the rate of growth of the economy under Labour was a mere 2.5 per cent a year.

The trade unions were angrily aware that employers had benefited considerably from these interventions, and that state investments were being used to save costs rather than to increase output. Clive Jenkins argued that the 'rationalisations' promoted by the IRC had led to the destruction of many jobs in industries where reorganisation had not been accompanied by increased demand.[24] But neither he nor the TUC argued against mergers or productivity deals. They continued to believe that growth could be achieved through modernisation and higher productivity, if only the government would adopt more expansionist policies. As the TUC document of 1968 (quoted on p. 70, above) asserted, a higher rate of growth could be built on a combination of increases in productivity and an expansion of the workforce.

Yet by the end of the period of Labour government in 1970, there was clear evidence that productivity and growth were not necessarily linked − indeed there was a strong negative correlation. While output was increasing fairly satisfactorily between 1962 and 1966, productivity increased slowly. When growth slowed down, productivity accelerated. On the other hand, productivity and unemployment were positively correlated. Between 1963 and 1966, when employment was increasing, productivity grew slowly; when productivity grew more rapidly, unemployment too rose sharply. There were important clues to the problems of the 1970s.

(v) Results of Labour's economic policies

In spite of the government's plans to promote growth, expansion was actually slower during this period than in the previous six years. Of all the targets set, only the one for productivity was approached; in fact, towards the end of the period productivity was growing faster than the planned rate. Between 1968 and 1971, GDP was growing at 2 per cent (compared with the 4 per cent projected by the 1965 Plan) whereas productivity in production industries was growing 3 per cent (compared with the 3.5 per cent target of the 1965 Plan) – in 1970-1 it increased by 4.1 per cent.

Of the three themes of Labour's original programme, productivity emerged as the strongest. Planning was largely discredited after the failure of 1965-6. Modernisation was still an aim, but limited by the slow expansion of investment as a result of cuts in the public sector. Productivity could be improved through the modernisation that did take place, but also as part of the restriction of prices and incomes. Trade unions were persuaded to use improvement in productivity in pay bargaining.

The aim of government policy was to promote productivity through the faster introduction of new technology. The effect of policy was to reinforce the factors contributing to the 'Ricardo phenomenon'. This was already an era of rapid technological innovation; policy was aimed at speeding it up. There was already a trend towards a decline in the productive workforce; policy on productivity reinforced that trend. It was already a period of slow growth of output; government fears about the balance of payments slowed it further. Thus the three elements in Ricardo's formula were strengthened to hasten the replacement of workers by new techniques, without corresponding increases of spendable earnings for the working class.

After the devaluation of 1967, the government concentrated on improving the balance of payments and controlling prices and incomes. There was no very strong reason, apart from this official caution, why output should not grow more quickly than it did. There were 0.5 million unemployed workers to absorb into the economy. But firms introduced new methods of production in ways that saved costs rather than increased output. New technology was substituted for workers, rather than used to supplement the productivity of the existing workforce.

Ricardo warned that this would tend to happen if entrepreneurs regarded labour costs as high. The prices and incomes policy encouraged employers to think of labour as costly, and to think of ways of economising on it. The same policies encouraged trade unions to bargain away jobs, but to expect longer-term improvements in earnings. Towards the end of the period this led to pressure for larger wage increases, which in turn led employers to seek other savings in labour costs.

Turner and Wilkinson showed that the average wage-earner's income, after tax, increased by only about 9.5 per cent during the Labour government's term of office. It thus grew more slowly than the economy as a whole, and far more slowly than productivity. This helps explain the growing hostility of the trade union movement to the Labour government towards the end of its term of office, and the strong opinion in trade union circles that prices and incomes policy was working against the interests of the working class.

The consequences for social policy of these developments were equally important. The Labour government moved significantly away from the principles of Beveridge, and towards the use of means-tested benefits as a method of relieving poverty. These will be dealt with in detail in a later chapter.

4 Economic policy 1970-9

The history of economic policy in Britain in the 1970s is dominated by the Heath government's attempt at expansion, and its aftermath. No post-war Chancellor of the Exchequer has been so universally condemned by economists as Anthony Barber. His policies have been described as rash to the point of irresponsibility, and the subsequent Labour government both saw itself and was seen as rescuing Britain from the combined effects of his actions, and the world recession which followed the oil price rises.

In this chapter, I shall show that the Heath government's policies can only be understood in the light of the 'Ricardo phenomenon'. In any other light they appear almost insane. It is hardly likely that a Conservative administration would cheerfully destroy the profitability of private industry and engineer record inflation through massive increases in public spending — unless it was in the grip of some form of collective economic madness. I shall demonstrate that these consequences followed from a new economic situation in which well-tried Conservative measures were no longer effective, and that the government, far from being insanely innovatory, was attempting economic expansion through traditional means. I shall also show that it was the Labour government that started to depart from post-war orthodoxies, by returning to the economic policies of the 1920s and 1930s.

(i) Heath's attempted expansion

The main accusations against the Heath administration are that it allowed investment in industry to fall disastrously; that it allowed the surplus of our exports of manufactured goods over imports of

77

such goods to decline by almost 50 per cent; that it allowed an expansion of the social services which was out of all proportion to Britain's industrial performance, and that it expanded the money supply so rapidly that it produced record inflation. Yet the declared aims of the Conservative government were entirely traditional. It came to office determined to produce economic growth through market forces, and to control public spending. It was forced to use public spending to stimulate expansion because no other measures would produce more output, and because unemployment kept rising in spite of monetary and fiscal measures to increase demand.

When the Labour government lost the election, it left the economy apparently poised for fairly rapid growth. Accordingly, the new Chancellor set about trying to achieve this according to Conservative election pledges. He cut income tax in his first budget; he cut purchase tax three months later; he cut the Bank Rate by 2 per cent in six months. Yet the output of productive industry increased by only 0.1 per cent between 1970 and 1971, and by only 2.2 per cent between 1971 and 1972. Meanwhile, unemployment increased from 600,000 at the beginning of 1971 to over 900,000 at the start of 1972. In other words, the combination of static output and rising redundancies defeated orthodox Conservative attempts at growth.

Furthermore, although investment in the public sector at this time was low, Bacon and Eltis concede that 'investment was not low in manufacturing',[1] and there was a near-record improvement in productivity of almost 5 per cent in productive industry in 1971-2. The government rapidly changed its public spending plans as a last resort when all other means of increasing employment and national income had been tried and failed.

The Conservative government took its responsibilities towards private industry very seriously, and imported the ex-director-general of the Confederation of British Industries (who had no political experience) into the Cabinet. Its very rapid expansion of the money supply from 1971 onwards was intended to help British industry, by making more credit available for investment, and by increasing demand. If expansion of industrial output had been profitable, this policy would clearly have produced both investment and growth. Instead, firms used the new money available to buy into real estate and buildings, and this property speculation produced an enormous rise in the price of land, houses and offices. Private investment grew rapidly, as intended, but it was not investment in industry.

Hence the common accusation that the Heath government *caused* industrial profit to collapse is quite unjustified. Ever since the mid-1960s, industry had found it more profitable to increase productivity than to increase output. Productivity was already growing at a rapid rate, and there was a limit to how fast it could improve. Businessmen still considered that it was unlikely to be profitable to employ more workers and to expand production. Hence they defeated government's attempts to stimulate growth by seeking other more profitable investments.

All the other failures of the Conservative measures followed from this fresh manifestation of the 'Ricardo phenomenon'. Because industrial output did not increase rapidly enough between 1970 and 1972, imports grew far too quickly as more money became available. Because employment in productive industry went on declining between 1970 and 1972, the government was trapped into providing more and more employment in the public sector – against all its intentions and plans. The oil price crisis was the final blow.

It is important to note that throughout the Heath administration, incomes of productive workers rose only very slowly, and from 1973 onwards they started to decline. Bacon and Eltis show that the proportion of industrial production consumed by industrial workers declined from 16.5 per cent in 1970 to 16.2 per cent in 1973; and it fell more rapidly after that. In 1962, industrial workers had consumed 17.3 per cent of industrial production. In other words, British industry was distributing a lower and lower proportion of its product to its workers, both during 'boom' conditions, and as part of a long-term trend. This helps to explain the militancy of opposition to incomes policies.

After 1975, the Labour government aimed at restoring the profitability of British industry, which was considered to have been destroyed by the policies of the Heath administration. However, because output still did not expand, this meant that the government had to take measures which further reduced employment, and diminished the share of production going to workers. The Conservatives had believed that growth and full employment were still possible, and that workers could benefit from expansion. Labour abandoned full-employment policies, cut public spending, and accepted the priorities of private industry – saving labour costs.

The way in which these developments unfolded can be better seen by a more detailed consideration of events in the 1970s.

(ii) The U-turns of the Heath government

It is well known that the Conservative government of 1970-4 did an about-turn in its economic policies about eighteen months after taking office. However, the full extent of the reversal of its declared priorities can only be appreciated by examining its pledges to the electorate.

In its election manifesto of 1970 the Conservative Party insisted that[2]

> under Labour, there has been too much government interference in the day-to-day workings of industry and local government. There has been too much government: there will be less. . . . We will reduce the number of civil servants. . . . The functions and responsibilities of all departments and government agencies will be systematically rationalised. There will be cost-reduction plans for every single Ministry in Whitehall, and the widespread application throughout government of the most modern management, budgeting and cost-effectiveness techniques.

The Conservatives claimed that they could restore a faster rate of growth by cutting taxation and allowing market prices free rein.[3]

> We will concentrate on making progressive and substantial reductions in income tax and surtax. These reductions will be possible because we will cut out unnecessary government spending and because we will encourage savings. . . . Our policies for strengthening competition will help keep down prices in the shops. Our policies for cutting taxes, for better industrial relations, for greater retraining, for improved efficiency in government and industry – all these will help stimulate output. This faster growth will mean that we can combine higher wages with steadier prices to bring a real increase in living standards.

The Conservatives rejected both Labour's adherence to government agencies' interventions to promote modernisation of industry and its prices and incomes policies.[4]

> We reject the detailed intervention of Socialism which usurps the functions of management and seeks to dictate prices and earnings in industry. . . . Our aim is to identify and remove obstacles that

prevent effective competition and restrict initiative. . . . We will repeal the so-called Industrial Expansion Act which gives the Government power to use taxpayers' money to buy its way into private industry. . . . We will drastically modify the Industrial Reorganisation Corporation Act. . . . The bureaucratic burden imposed upon industry by government departments, agencies and boards has steadily increased in recent years. We will see that it is reduced.

The manifesto was prefaced by a note from Mr Heath himself, pledging that the Conservatives would not, as Labour had done, change their minds about policies at the first hint of opposition or adversity.[5]

once a decision is made, once a policy is established, the Prime Minister and his colleagues should have the courage to stick to it. Nothing has done Britain more harm in the world than the endless backing and filling which we have seen in recent years. . . . At the first sign of difficulties the Labour Government has sounded the retreat, covering its withdrawal with a smokescreen of unlikely excuses. But courage and intellectual honesty are essential qualities in politics, and in the interest of our country it is high time that we saw them again.

This pledge was particularly unfortunate in view of the speed with which the new government changed its mind on many of these issues. As promised, it did amalgamate ministries and disband a number of agencies, notably the Industrial Reorganisation Corporation and the Prices and Incomes Board. However, even as it was doing so, it was already being drawn into the kind of intervention that it had criticised in its predecessors. In November 1970, a grant of £42 million was announced to Rolls Royce for the development of the RB-211 engine. This was consistent with the manifesto's assertion that 'specific projects . . . will continue to be given Government support.'[6] But two months later the government had to intervene again, and go right against its declared policies by partially nationalising the company. In June 1971, it was again drawn into intervention, this time in Upper Clyde Shipbuilders, and after lengthy negotiations made a loan of £35 million to enable the company to be taken over by a private firm. In both these examples, the political and social consequences of allowing 'lame ducks' to perish were counted far too serious for a declared policy to be maintained.

Far more dramatic was the government's change of direction over incomes policy. Alarmed by the consequences of confrontation with the public sector workers over pay claims – and particularly by the miners' strike of January 1972 – the government entered into lengthy negotiations with the TUC and CBI, aimed at getting an agreement about general levels of pay increases. When these failed to produce a system of voluntary restraint, the government announced a compulsory freeze in November 1972. Phase II of the new policy (aimed at restricting wage increases to a maximum of £1 per week plus 4 per cent of the average wage bill for the workers concerned) was greeted with hostility by the unions the following spring, but was fairly successful, mainly because the economy was at last growing fairly rapidly, and unemployment had begun to fall. However, towards the end of the year, sharp increases in prices coincided with the introduction of Phase III which restricted wage increases to 7 per cent on basic rates, plus certain additions for efficiency or 'unsocial hours'. When the miners refused to accept an offer in line with this norm, and again went on strike, in February 1974, the government called a general election. The defeat of the Conservatives could largely be attributed to the failure of the incomes policy.

However, the less spectacular but more fundamental change in Conservative policy was over public expenditure. In line with election pledges, the government's public expenditure White Paper, published in January 1971, announced that spending in 1974-5 would be about £950 million lower than Labour had planned. But as unemployment figures went on rising throughout 1971, the next White Paper, published that November, raised spending plans for 1974-5 by nearly £500 million. In fact, so rapidly was the government changing its mind that even larger increases had already been announced by then, and by December 1972 the government was planning to spend a further £1,200 million in that year over and above the previous increase.

Thus it was during the latter half of 1971 that the Conservative administration started to be alarmed about the failure of all its other measures to reduce unemployment, and hastily resorted to public spending as a way of providing jobs as well as of increasing demand. The rise in GDP of 6.3 per cent which took place between 1972 and 1973 could be attributed to this expansion, which increased public expenditure by 5.2 per cent in 1971-2, by 6.6 per cent in 1972-3 and by 8.4 per cent in 1973-4, and its proportion of GDP from 51 per cent to 58 per cent during the Conservatives' term of office. The government lost its nerve when faced with the prospect of over a million unemployed, and an even poorer record of growth than its predecessor. To achieve its modest reduction in unemployment, it had to stand its policies on their heads.

It also had to allow the money supply to grow far more rapidly than originally intended, and to raise the Public Sector Borrowing Requirement to record levels. As inflation became an increasingly worrying problem, members of the Conservative Party were quick to criticise government policy. There was always a strong monetarist minority among the party's MPs. In the debate on Mr Barber's first 'mini-budget', in October 1970, the Chairman of the Conservative Finance Committee, Peter Hordern, bitterly attacked the Governor of the Bank of England for allowing the money supply to grow far more rapidly before and after the election than the Labour Chancellor's budget guidelines had suggested. 'Inflation is much too important to leave to such a Governor,' he declared.[7] When the government enforced a prices and incomes freeze, the economic radicals, headed by a Conservative MP, wrote the Prime Minister an open letter arguing that inflation had nothing to do with wage rises, and urging the case for cuts in the money supply, as well as increased taxes or reductions in public expenditure.[8] The government was also heavily criticised for its interventions into industry. In the debate on the Rolls Royce rescue, Enoch Powell intoned:[9]

> This is an extraordinary proposition to come from a Conservative Government, that state ownership is the natural instrument, the chosen method, for restoring unprofitable assets to profitability. By this decision the Government have done a grave wrong.

In retrospect, the radical Right — including members of the Heath Cabinet like Sir Keith Joseph and Margaret Thatcher, who had severe doubts about the reversal of economic policies at the time — were able to recognise that fears over the issue of unemployment were far less justified than doubts about incomes policy. The government got relatively little trouble from the trade unions over unemployment, and little gratitude for its efforts to give priority to the low paid. It started to lose ground over pay awards in the public sector, and finally collapsed over Phase III. With hindsight, Conservatives recognised that they might have done better to stick to their guns, to have concentrated on controlling public spending and reducing taxation, and to have worried less about higher unemployment — which might indeed have been used as a weapon to moderate wage increases.

(iii) The Labour government 1974-9

During the period of the Conservative administration, the Labour leadership set about rebuilding its relationship with the trade union movement, which had crumbled towards the end of its previous term of office. The result was the 'Social Contract', which heavily influenced Labour's platform in the two elections of 1974.

Compared with previous manifestos, the Labour Party's in February 1974 gave much greater emphasis to social policy. After defining the current crisis in terms of inflation, unemployment, oil prices and Common Market membership, the manifesto set out a policy on energy, based on expanding coal production and nationalising North Sea Oil, and then made a number of specific pledges in relation to pensioners, the disabled, child benefits and housing, which represented the substance of the Social Contract. The topic of 'Employment and Expansion' was relegated below this, and dealt mainly with increasing public ownership — a concession to the left wing of the party. The manifesto ended with a resounding summary of its[10]

socialist aims, and we are proud of the word. . . . It is indeed our intention to:

(a) bring about a fundamental and irreversible shift in the balance of power and wealth in favour of working people and their families;

(b) eliminate poverty wherever it exists in Britain, and commit ourselves to a substantial increase in our contribution to fight poverty abroad;

(c) make power in industry genuinely accountable to the workers and the community at large;

(d) achieve far greater economic equality — in income, wealth and living standards;

(e) increase social equality by giving far greater importance to full employment, housing, education and social benefits;

(f) improve the environment in which our people live and work and spend their leisure.

These intentions were as much renunciations of the previous Labour government's policies as they were denunciations of the Conservatives' record. This programme was as thoroughgoingly socialist as the Tories' had been radically right wing in the 1970 election. Yet the performance of the new government in office from the second 1974 election onwards was as unlike its declared intentions as the Conservative government's had been. The Labour government did immediately raise pensions, commit itself to a new pension scheme and higher child benefits, freeze rents, stabilise mortgage rates and subsidise food prices. But it also became embroiled in its usual anxieties about the balance of payments, and was quickly emphasising to the nation and the world that the energy crisis would prevent any growth or rise in living standards for several years. Speaking at the TUC conference at Brighton, just before the October election, Harold Wilson said:[11]

because of the crisis we face, including the oil surcharge, we cannot expect any increase in living standards overall in the next year or two; indeed it will be a tremendous challenge to our statesmanship even to maintain average living standards.

Accordingly, the second manifesto of 1974 placed greater emphasis on the economic crisis, the balance of payments problem and the difficult road ahead. While it still stressed the importance of the Social Contract, it gave priority to the control of inflation in economic affairs, and promoted its long-term plans for employment and expansion above its pledges on social justice. In a section which began 'In the long run, a nation, like a family, can only live on what it earns,' the manifesto described the objectives of its Industry Act, and the National Enterprise Board (NEB). A series of 'planning agreements' would be concluded between the government and the major industries, the NEB would take a shareholding in firms where this seemed necessary in order to promote investment or exports. These proposals were the new counterparts to the National Plan and the Industrial Reorganisation Corporation.

In practice, the NEB was not created until 1976, nor were any planning agreements made before its creation. By this time, the economic tide had turned strongly against the radicals in the government.

Tony Benn's actions during his brief period as Secretary of State for Industry were focused on giving assistance to firms threatened with closure as a result of the growing recession, rather than on promoting modernisation or expansion. He lost this post in 1975, and this meant that both key jobs in the sphere of economic policy were in the hands of 'moderates' — Denis Healey and Eric Varley — who had no great interest in pursuing the policies proclaimed in the manifesto. The NEB in turn was mainly used to rescue ailing companies rather than to extend nationalisation or promote growth — a trend already set by Eric Varley in 1975-6 with the £160 million rescue of Chrysler.

Meanwhile, Denis Healey's responses to the series of crises which beset the economy were eclectic. Faced, in 1974, with a balance of payments deficit of £4,000 million, an inflation rate of over 15 per cent and rising unemployment, he presented a budget in April that was, in effect, mildly deflationary. He judged that he could neither afford to adopt an orthodox Keynesian response to recession, nor an orthodox monetarist response to inflation. But he was forced by events to change tack frequently, introducing further measures in July and November. By April 1975, he was increasing income tax and other forms of taxation — acknowledging that the consequent reduction in demand would raise unemployment — and forecasting stricter control of public spending.

Throughout the first year of the new government, the notion of a statutory incomes policy had been rigorously avoided — in his memoirs, Harold Wilson refers to it as the 'ignis fatuus' of economic policy. But in June 1975, the Cabinet became alarmed at the inflation rate of 26 per cent, the continuing round of wage settlements at around 30 per cent, and the precarious state of the pound. Denis Healey announced that controls would be introduced unless a voluntary policy could be agreed. Within ten days, the TUC had made proposals for a limit on pay increases, and the government had published a White Paper, along very similar lines, suggesting a maximum of £6 a week for increases in the next year.

At this point, Labour's retreat from its socialist programme began to become as total as the Conservatives' from their manifesto. Ministers became convinced by the growing advice from economists that Britain's problem was of 'too few producers', and that the only solution was — somehow — to make the expansion of industrial production profitable once more. This was reflected in speeches made in 1976 by the Labour leadership. On 25 February 1976, Denis Healey announced that[12]

The TUC and the Labour party are united in believing that the steady contraction in our manufacturing industry is the main reason for our disappointing economic performance since the war. This contraction must be halted and reversed. But we cannot reverse the trend if we plan to take more resources into the public services. . . . In recent years our competitors have increased the manpower in their manufacturing industry; we have seen a massive shift of manpower out of manufacturing into the public services. . . . We cannot afford to continue eroding the foundation of our prosperity in this way.

As public expenditure was cut and unemployment rose, the new Prime Minister, James Callaghan, spelt out that the strengthening of the economy's market sector was the means by which the government was seeking any future expansion. In a reply to a question in the House of Commons, on 27 April, he emphasised,

It is important that productive jobs should be created and that we should rely on investments on which a successful return can be expected. That is the way to achieve more employment rather than by transferring more and more jobs to the public sector.

Conservative members cheered this announcement that the Labour government's main priority would be restoring the profits of private industry.

By this time, however, the government had recognised to some extent one of the indications of the 'Ricardo phenomenon'. Increased investment would only produce growth and ultimately more employment if it was aimed at higher output, rather than higher productivity alone. Industry could only be persuaded that it would be profitable to invest for expansion if it could be convinced that demand would grow, and labour costs would fall, or at least remain steady. To achieve this, government had to co-operate with industry in holding down the incomes of the working class.

The incomes policy was one means by which this was achieved, by restricting wage increases to £4 a week during Phase II. But the government particularly wanted to increase exports, and hence aimed to reduce British labour costs in relation to those of Britain's competitors. Bacon and Eltis suggest that the government engineered the fall in the value of the pound, in the spring of 1976, precisely to cut the wages of

British workers in dollar terms. An effective devaluation of 15 per cent against the dollar took place in 1976:[13]

> As British wages only rose about 12 per cent in the year from
> March 1976 until March 1977, while wages in other leading indus-
> trial countries rise at an annual rate of near to 10 per cent, the
> objective of cutting wage costs per unit of output in relation to
> those of Britain's leading competitors by 10 per cent or more was
> certainly achieved.

However, the final two years of the Labour government, like those of its predecessor of 1966 to 1970, were dominated by the growing antagonism of workers to attempts to restrict their earnings, and criticisms from the left wing of the party over controls on government spending. Once again, in 1979, the claim to have 'made the pound strong' was not enough to satisfy disgruntled former supporters.

The final paradox of economic policy was the fact that Denis Healey's later policies anticipated the monetarist orthodoxies of the Conservatives. As a member of his own parliamentary party later wrote,[14]

> it was not the Conservatives in government who first denounced
> Keynes and embraced Friedman. It was not Mrs. Thatcher but Jim
> Callaghan as Prime Minister, who declared that we could no longer
> spend our way out of a slump, if we ever could. It was Denis Healey,
> not Geoffrey Howe, who first put monetarism onto the agenda of
> British politics, and abandoned a Keynesian strategy. It was Healey,
> not Howe, who put prices and profits before public spending and
> jobs. It was Healey, not Howe, who first stressed the need for confi-
> dence and management incentives, rather than planning and public
> enterprise, as the vehicles of resource allocation. In short, it was
> hardly surprising that the last time round the electors were confused
> on which twin was the credible Tory.

Stuart Holland went on to argue that there is now a monetarist consensus between the right wings of the two major parties.

In its efforts to improve the profitability of industry and increase industrial investment, the Labour government did indeed adopt Conservative policies — but it was the Conservatism of an earlier era, and not that of Edward Heath. The Labour government set aside any

attempt at full employment. It concentrated on investment in high-technology industry, which was considered to be more profitable, and paid no heed to issues of employment.

A good example of Labour's new priorities is to be found in energy policy. The government continued to develop the high-technology nuclear power industry, with its very small labour force. It also invested

Table 4.1 Gross Domestic Capital Formation at 1975 prices (£m.)

	1973	*1974*	*1975*	*1976*	*1977*	*1978*
Petroleum and natural gas	309	707	1,348	1,857	1,731	1,626

heavily in North Sea Oil and gas. The increase in investment in these enterprises can be seen from the figures given in Table 4.1.[15] By contrast, investment in the more labour-intensive coalmining industry increased much more slowly, in spite of enormous rises in output and productivity in the late 1970s (see Table 4.2).

Table 4.2 Investment and output in mining and quarrying

	1973	*1974*	*1975*	*1976*	*1977*	*1978*	*1979*
Gross capital formation (£m.) at 1975 prices	148	173	201	248	272	360	not available
Index of output (1975 = 100)	110.1	89.9	100.0	125.8	187.7	232.5	294.7
Index of output per person employed (1975 = 100)	107.1	90.5	100.0	127.2	189.8	238.7	307.0

It is difficult to resist the conclusion that the government preferred to develop sources of energy which relied relatively little on labour, and more on capital, because of the experiences of its predecessors in the miners' strike. From the point of view of social and economic control, high-technology production of energy provided government with better means of regulating its sources of supply.

If the regional pattern of employment in Britain in the 1970s is examined, the power of the 'Ricardo phenomenon' to resist government policies can be more fully appreciated. In spite of the Heath government's attempts at reducing unemployment, the total number of male employees in employment fell in all the industrial regions in the 1970s, including the prosperous South-East. The only regions

Table 4.3 Male employees in employment (thousands)

	1968	1969	1970	1971	1972	1973	1974	1975	1976	1977	1978	1979
South-East	4,574	4,538	4,464	4,412	4,392	4,394	4,347	4,291	4,243	not available as separate figures		
East Anglia	387	394	395	383	391	403	404	406	405			
South-West	923	899	901	895	899	920	913	906	894	904	910	910
West Midlands	1,450	1,441	1,427	1,393	1,364	1,390	1,372	1,350	1,325	1,337	1,337	1,318
East Midlands	928	923	910	888	887	905	898	896	900	908	907	904
Yorks and Humberside	1,280	1,270	1,247	1,212	1,200	1,218	1,214	1,205	1,191	1,205	1,199	1,196
North-West	1,712	1,695	1,663	1,623	1,598	1,611	1,600	1,572	1,543	1,541	1,530	1,514
North	805	795	798	772	763	779	768	774	769	768	762	761
Wales	663	650	636	629	630	636	621	618	612	611	609	610
Scotland	1,290	1,286	1,267	1,216	1,194	1,221	1,227	1,219	1,210	1,203	1,203	1,199
Northern Ireland	292	293	295	290	289	293	296	293	291	not available		

in which the total number of male employees in employment increased
were rural ones – East Anglia and the South-West (see Table 4.3).[16]
  The effects on incomes of Labour's policies are clear from the figures
given in Table 4.4 of average weekly earnings of full-time male manual
workers in manufacturing and certain other industries.[17]

Table 4.4

	1974	1975	1976	1977	1978
Average earnings (£, at 1975 prices)	60.04	59.58	57.98	54.80	57.99

(iv) Policy in the 1970s

Some commentators have suggested that the tendency in the 1970s
of governments to abandon their pre-election programmes within
two years of taking office was a consequence of our political system.
For instance, Stewart has argued that[18]

> Both Labour and Conservative parties, while in opposition, have
> succumbed to the temptation to condemn a large proportion of the
> government's policies and have promised to reverse many of these
> policies when they themselves took office. The result has been a
> fatal lack of continuity.

He names this the Jekyll-and-Hyde syndrome, and suggested that
'U-turns' were in fact evidence of coming to terms with reality – but
that by this time damage had been done by reckless or irrelevant
measures.
  This seems a shallow interpretation of events, that does no justice
to underlying economic problems. The Heath government came to
power convinced that it could promote faster growth by less intervention and allowing market prices freer rein. The main cause of its
change of policy was high rates of unemployment and continued low
rates of growth. The trend of the previous five years towards increased
mechanisation and redundancy without increased output continued
under the Conservatives despite new policies. Alarmed by growing
unemployment they chose to increase public spending in dramatic
and unprecedented ways in an attempt to overcome this trend, and

failed. Labour inherited the aftermath of this failure, and tried to do something about the social consequences of the problem, raising benefits and child allowances. But they in turn lost their nerve in face of pressure on sterling, and reverted to a managerial style of politics, characteristic of the embattled Wilson and Callaghan, using monetarist measures of restraint, cutting government spending and controlling incomes.

The counterpart to the Conservatives' desensitisation to rapid expansion of public spending was Labour's heightened tolerance of a rising rate of unemployment. Under the Labour government of 1966-70, 0.5 million unemployed (the prospect of which had frightened their Tory predecessors in 1963) became an accepted fact of everyday life. The Labour government of 1974-9 made 1 million unemployed an acceptable level. In reading Harold Wilson's memoirs, one is struck by his continuous anxiety about sterling and the balance of payments, which contrasts with a resigned fatalism about lengthening dole queues. Yet Labour's manifesto of 1974, while it made no promises about full employment, did commit the party to a programme of reducing unemployment figures. Under Wilson, Callaghan and Healey, the way was prepared for the Conservatives to adopt policies which frankly admitted that unemployment would be increased, at least in the short run.

Another important change that occurred under Labour was that the Manpower Services Commission's role came to be as much about 'job creation' as about retraining workers from old and declining industries for new and expanding ones. Under Labour in the 1960s, the emphasis was all on modernisation and redeployment to more productive jobs; in the 1970s it shifted to the provision of certain kinds of socially useful, though non-commercial, employment, and subsidised work-experience for unemployed teenagers. Inevitably, this meant that state-financed employment schemes were in very low-productivity occupations — at the opposite end of the economic scale from the supposed aim of retraining. Government hence reinforced the growing split between high-productivity, automated industry, and the sector of employment that could not effectively modernise, and where incomes consequently lagged behind.

Yet, in spite of low investment and growth, productivity improved more rapidly in the 1970s than in the 1960s, except in the period 1974-5, when the recession was at its worst. During the nine years 1970-9, GDP per person employed grew by 14.2 per cent, an annual average of 1.6 per cent. But in the production industries, output per person employed increased by 22.4 per cent, or 2.5 per cent a year — in spite of a substantial fall in productivity in 1974 and 1975. Towards the end of the period, the improvements in output per person employed in the production industries were considerable (see Table 4.5).

Table 4.5

	1975	*1976*	*1977*	*1978*	*1979*
Index of output per person employed in production industries (1975 = 100)	100.0	103.5	108.1	113.5	117.4

This represents an annual increase in productivity of 3.7 per cent — faster than the target rate of the 1965 National Plan. Yet, in the same period, output of production industries grew by only 2.2 per cent a year.

Both Labour and Conservative governments put heavy emphasis on the crisis over Middle-East oil prices as a cause of the failure of their policies. Yet, as I have shown in the last chapter, the underlying trends towards lower growth, higher unemployment, but increased productivity, were all present before 1974. High oil prices accentuated the balance of payments problem, and the world reaction to them in turn reinforced our recession — but all this merely added to the type of crisis (and government response to it) that had occurred in 1966. The stop-go policies of the Conservatives, in the 1950s and early 1960s, were caricatured by the extremes of recklessness and restraint of governments in the 1970s, not because of the extremism of their views so much as the inadequacy of their weapons to tackle the underlying problems of the economy.

Thus Stewart's suggestion that governments tended to start with doctrinaire notions and quickly revert to a more rational 'middle way' in economic affairs, is not borne out by the facts. A more accurate summary of economic policy in the 1970s would be that both Keynesian methods and monetarist ones were tried without success — and that, paradoxically, it was a Conservative government that was drawn into Keynesian policies and a Labour one that reluctantly tried a monetarist approach. The difference was that Heath's combination of rapid increases in public spending and a statutory incomes policy was a fairly thoroughgoing version of Keynesian measures, whereas Labour's monetarism was less wholehearted. Consequently, the Conservatives could argue that the monetarist approach had not been given a fair trial, and that a longer period of more drastic measures to cut public spending and control the money supply should be tried. I shall examine the implications of this in the next chapter.

5 The new Conservatism

(i) The conversion of the Conservatives

In what turned out to be an epoch-making speech in September 1974, Sir Keith Joseph attacked the recently defeated Heath government (in which he had been Secretary of State for Health and Social Security) for over-reacting to short-term unemployment figures, and allowing the money supply to expand too rapidly. Harking back to the Conservative manifesto of 1970, he reminded his party that they had been pledged to less intervention by the state, to greater scope for market forces, and to controlling public expenditure. But in restating the tenets of the Selsdon Conference of 1970, he placed a far harsher stress on monetary control, and the acceptance of its social consequences, than had been heard from a leading Conservative spokesman since the war:[1]

> The effect of over-reacting to temporary recessions has been to push up inflation to even higher levels, not to help the unemployed, but to increase their numbers. . . . If policies are to be judged by the criterion of the greatest good of the greatest number, then excessive expansion of the money supply has been found wholly wanting, in practice and theory alike.

Sir Keith Joseph insisted that unemployment statistics were misleading, and that only a minority could be regarded as genuinely unemployed. The rest were either briefly between jobs, too infirm to work, or scroungers. Instead of trying artificially to reduce unemployment statistics through budget deficits, government should concentrate on restoring 'sound money', by restricting increases in the money supply to a small and regular amount each year. This was the only way to ensure stable prices, a steady growth of the economy, and as full employment as could be maintained in the long term.

At the time, Sir Keith Joseph's arguments (which he carried forward the following month in a speech in which he seemed to recommend compulsory birth control for the lowest social classes) appeared much too extreme and abrasive to be accepted by his party, let alone the electorate. Yet within six months the Conservative leadership had been seized by his protégée, Margaret Thatcher, and the party's policies had swung suddenly from compromise to confrontation, from neo-Keynesian to monetarist principles.

Although monetarism focuses on inflation as its main target, unemployment is a key element in its analysis of economic problems. In their arguments with Keynesians, monetarists have always insisted that prices can rise only if the supply of money is increased to pay for them. In the early 1970s, the standard monetarist argument was that governments used public spending programmes recklessly to try to promote growth and reduce unemployment; but that this increased money more than it expanded industrial output, so prices rose faster. In Sir Keith Joseph's original model, government had only to learn to tolerate the 'natural' level of unemployment, and to control the growth of its own spending in line with the expansion in the rest of the economy, for inflation to be curbed.

However, under Labour from 1976 to 1979, unemployment rose to double the figure for 1974, when Sir Keith Joseph was speaking, and public spending was cut; yet inflation continued (at a reduced rate), and growth was only modest. In government, the Conservative leadership now insists that we must have even higher unemployment, and even bigger public-spending cuts. The key to this apparent extremism is the problem of economic growth. The monetarist remedy for inflation and stagnation cannot work unless wages actually *fall* in real value, rather than simply cease to rise in money terms; and the key to a reduction in wages is seen as a very high rate of unemployment. This in turn can only be achieved by an increase in bankruptcies, and the closure of firms.

Monetarism does address itself to the 'Ricardo phenomenon', but in a somewhat paradoxical way. I have suggested that growth slows down or stops when a country reaches a certain point of industrialisation, because there are insufficient workers in low-productivity, non-industrial jobs to absorb into new industrial jobs. Bacon and Eltis have called the process that occurs when absolute automation starts to take place 'de-industrialisation' — by which they mean that productive industry employs fewer *workers*. But under the new Conservative government, de-industrialisation has meant fewer factories as well. Its policies seem to be based on the notion that, at some point in the downward slide of factories closing and dole queues lengthening, wages will be forced down to a level at which firms will start to expand employment. Another way of putting this would be that if the clock is turned back far enough, and Britain reverts to conditions as they were before it became fully industrialised, there will be a chance to industrialise all over again.

It is impossible to tell how this process might work, or whether it could work at all. Britain is the first country to reach the stage of absolute automation, so there are no precedents on which to base predictions. What is clear is that Conservative policies are reinforcing all the factors in the 'Ricardo phenomenon' that I have identified so far. At the time of writing, unemployment is over 2 million, and industrial production is lower than in 1975 (which in turn was considerably lower than in 1973), and falling. Wages are failing to keep pace with inflation. Bacon and Eltis have shown that, since 1964, industrial workers have consumed a lower and lower proportion of industrial production; this process is accelerating as employment shrinks and real wages fall. As the government is also committed, through its Employment Act, to regulating industrial action, the shape of future working-class resistance to these attacks on living standards is unclear. The politics of this process will be discussed in Part 4 of this book. But in economic terms, no one can guess how low wages have to fall before employers start to see labour as a more attractive factor of production. What is clear is that, in the process of trying to force wages down, the government will also force output down, and produce a recession of unprecedented proportions in the post-war era. Thus output cannot start to expand, according to present predictions, until unemployment reaches about 3 million people.

(ii) Monetarist theories of growth

Theorists of the monetarist school make it clear that they consider that Keynesian policies have, over the past forty years, so distorted the economy that only a drastic reallocation of resources can allow growth. They argue that wages have been allowed to rise artificially, and inefficient companies have been kept in business, through Keynesian budget deficits, and that the necessary restoration of competition and the price mechanism will involve painful doses of unemployment and bankruptcy.

For instance, F.A. von Hayek, one of the gurus of the new Conservatism, and a contemporary critic of Keynes, consistently predicted that the system of monetary expansion and increased public spending as a means to growth would collapse. In the 1920s and 1930s he argued that the depression reflected a maldistribution of production between industries, and not a failure of demand. He criticised Keynes's assumption that, for political reasons, no wage could be lowered, and that, consequently, expenditure had to be raised sufficiently to take up the whole supply of labour at current wage rates. He insisted that this simply perpetuated the maldistribution of labour between industries, and that it would result in unemployment as soon as inflation was curbed.

Ever since the 1930s, Hayek has continued to maintain that Keynesian policies prolonged this distortion, and created a vicious circle. There was a sector of the economy that was inefficient and unprofitable and that could only survive by still further artificial support — either through direct injections of credit, or by expansions of the money supply to pay uneconomic wages, and to create demand at unrealistic prices. This process became cumulative over time, he argued. To maintain an artificially high level of employment, the government had to expand the supply of money more and more, since inefficient industries were less and less able to compete. This was the real explanation not only of the continuous post-war inflation, but also of low rates of growth. Resources that should be redeployed in efficient businesses were being wastefully retained in outmoded ones. The longer this went on, the harsher would be the result when the collapse came, and the more painful the process of reallocation.

Hayek argues that, by expanding the supply of money faster than output, government has removed from firms and from workers the twin responsibilities of being profitable and of preventing unemployment. He rejects the notion that the money supply increases because of higher costs (for instance, of raw materials):[2]

To this claim it must be replied emphatically that, in the strict sense, there is simply no such thing as a 'cost-push' inflation. Neither

higher wages nor higher prices of oil, or perhaps of imports generally, can drive up the aggregate price of all goods *unless the pur-*
chasers are given more money to buy them. What is called a cost-
push inflation is merely the effect of increases in the quantity of
money which governments feel forced to provide in order to prevent
unemployment resulting from a rise in wages (or other costs), which
preceded it and which was conceded in the expectation that governments would increase the quantity of money. They mean thereby to
make it possible for all the workers to find employment through a
rise in the demand for their products. If government did not increase
the quantity of money such a rise in the wages of a group of workers
would not lead to a rise in the general price level, but simply to a
reduction in sales and therefore to unemployment.

Hayek restates Ricardo's view that recession is a consequence of the
fact that too many of some goods are being produced, and too few of
others. Growth can only restart when the right proportions of production between commodities are restored. Employment cannot, in the
long run, be a function of total demand – this is an example of a
Keynesian 'fallacy of aggregates'. Since Keynes, expenditure has been
increased to maintain that part of employment that will depend on
still further expenditure. The only sound way to adjust the labour force
between industries is through the structure of relative wages, respond-
ing in turn to continuous changes in the direction of demand. Thus,
falling wages and unemployment signal decreasing demand, and a need
to shift production to other industries, where demand for both labour
and production is increasing.

Though the pessimistic side of Hayek's analysis seems to have been
amply justified by events in the 1970s, the optimistic parts of his prescriptions are not so clearly indicated. We have seen that Ricardo's
model of growth depended heavily on the notion of a large rural
sector of the economy, where wages and productivity were low, and a
rapidly expanding urban and industrial sector with a growing demand
for labour, and where wages and productivity were higher. When
Ricardo wrote of a maldistribution of production between different
types of employment he was thinking primarily of the different proportions of workers in very labour-intensive employment (agricultural
and hand-made production) and the more capital-intensive industries.
He also assumed a rising population, with rising demand for manufactured products, and the availability of export markets.

None of these conditions now exist. Far from increasing its work-force, manufacturing industry is reducing it, and this trend has recently continued even when output was being expanded. Technological change has indeed continued to create wide gaps between the productivity of different sectors of the labour force, but it has not created a demand for increased labour. Thus there is no obvious source of growth, either in employment or output, to be obtained by redeploying labour from one sector to another, such as existed in the nineteenth century. Demand is unlikely to increase through population growth or through new export markets.

In other words, while Keynesian policies have probably contributed to the maintenance of employment in some old-fashioned and ineffic-ient industries, it seems very unlikely that monetarist policies will result in a major increase in employment in new and efficient ones. What does seem certain is that monetarist policies will force down some wages, and hugely increase unemployment. This may eventually result in a rise in employment in certain low-productivity, low-wage jobs (such as catering), where labour is already a major factor. But it is difficult to see how even a large pool of unemployed workers and a considerable drop in wages will make much difference to long-term plans in high-productivity, capital-intensive industries, where new technology is already causing the workforce to be contracted, not expanded.

(iii) The Conservatives in office

In the first year of the Conservative government, there were 212,933 redundancies and threatened redundancies, according to an analysis done by the *Sunday Times*.[3] There were thirty-four areas in which un-employment stood at over 12.5 per cent of the male workforce in June 1980. All but one of these were in Scotland, Wales, the North or South-West of England. In Glasgow, the unemployment rate was 12.4 per cent of the male workforce.[4]

In marked contrast with the Heath government, Mrs Thatcher's Cabinet has showed no signs of concern about rising unemployment. Replying to a question in the House of Commons on 24 June 1980, Mrs Thatcher remarked that, 'If our top priority is to squeeze inflation out of the economy, it is, sadly, inevitable that in the short run we shall suffer some unemployment.' In a debate on the economy, on 11

July, Sir Geoffrey Howe said that unemployment was 'bound to rise' as demand for British goods fell during the world recession, and one of his back-bench colleagues criticised the unemployed in the North of England (with a male unemployment rate of 11 per cent) for failing to move to the South-East, where the unemployment rate was a mere 5 per cent.

In line with the school of monetarist orthodoxy which has always insisted that unemployment was caused by wages being too high, Sir Keith Joseph, as Secretary of State for Industry, has maintained that only lower wages can reduce unemployment. Speaking on BBC Radio 4, on 29 June 1980, he suggested that a significant proportion of unemployment was actually voluntary, in the sense that jobs could be provided at lower rates of pay. He argued that it was in the interests of the workers to offer themselves to employers 'at a slightly lower unit labour cost figure'. He added, 'I want to emphasise that just as people can price themselves out of jobs, so they can price themselves into jobs.'[5]

With the annual rate of inflation running at around 20 per cent throughout their first year in office, the Conservatives had scope for reducing wages by holding money wage rises to something under that figure. In the 1920s and early 1930s, when similar orthodoxies prevailed, prices were falling, so that in order to achieve a 'slightly lower unit labour cost figure' (as Sir Keith Joseph so delicately puts it) money wages had actually to be reduced. Now the government's policies will have succeeded as long as wage increases can be held back below the rate of inflation; as indeed they were in the first quarter of 1980, when earnings after tax and inflation fell by 1.5 per cent.[6]

Conservative ministers have continued to urge improvements in productivity, and to refuse to recognise the connection between productivity deals and increased redundancies. When asked what he proposed to do about unemployment in the North-East of England, where he was visiting a factory on 11 July 1980, Sir Keith Joseph replied: 'If pay claims are accompanied by a willingness to co-operate via productivity, it is more likely that entrepreneurs from Britain and abroad will want to come to the area.'[7]

In fact, new technology continued to play almost as great a part in causing redundancies in the early months of the Conservative government as reductions in output. Out of 53,725 redundancies between 10 May and 10 September 1979, 19,790 were attributed to 'rationalisation', 'streamlining' or 'automation'.[8] In 1980, firms tended to attribute redundancies to falling orders, but, even so, ambitious new plans for automation were still going ahead. For instance, in June 1980, Ford announced plans for a major modernisation of their production methods. Under the headline 'Ford set course for robot future', the *Guardian* reported that[9]

> Ford management throughout Britain and Europe has been alerted by the company to prepare the way for a huge cost-saving exercise which could lead to radical changes on the shop floor and the loss of thousands of jobs. The plan scheduled for implementation over the next 10 years is expressly designed to meet the threat posed by the Japanese car industry, and entails the increasing use of robots, the elimination of many craft grades, and the introduction of supervisors on the production line wherever necessary.

The report makes it clear that Ford's emphasis will be cost-saving, and that the company's rules and procedures would have to be modified to accommodate the new plans: 'Technicians would be brought in to replace fitters and electricians, and the increasing use of robots would be allied to the interlinking of machines and loading and unloading by automation.'[10]

Yet Conservative government spokesmen still emphasise the importance of new technology in expanding output and creating new jobs. In face of massive evidence to the contrary, the Under-Secretary of State for Industry, Michael Marshall, told the House of Commons, on 11 July 1980, in a debate on the microelectronics industry, that microprocessors did not threaten jobs. He assured the House that, in his opinion, new technology for the storing and communication of information within and between offices was a growth industry, and that Britain could find new employment by the establishment of new firms producing microprocessors.[11] Ignoring the evidence that these industries are tending to develop in countries like Brazil and Taiwan where labour is cheaper, and that they are not, in any case, labour intensive, this also begs the question of the millions of office workers whose jobs are threatened by word-processors and other new information technology.

Yet within the Conservative Party outside government, there are MPs who have warned that there should be a long-term strategy to deal with the consequences of microtechnology. The few Conservative MPs who have computer experience, and who therefore appreciate the deeper implications of employing microelectronics, have criticised government short-sightedness and expediency. A working party was set up just before the 1979 election by Sir Keith Joseph, headed by Ian Lloyd, the computer-experienced MP for Havant and Waterloo, which published a report full of ideas repugnant to the Joseph philosophy.

The report proposed that the state, not the employer, should meet the costs of redundancies which it considered an inevitable consequence of information technology. Although equally committed to the expansion of the microprocessor industry, the report regarded the employment implications of technological change as far too important to leave to the free market, and suggested that only a commitment by government to assistance with these consequences would 'encourage intellectual and physical mobility and topple the barriers to change.'[12] Yet this sort of insight leads it authors to be classified as 'wets', at least on this issue, in the Conservative Party.

(iv) Economic prospects under the Conservatives

In June 1980, the Independent Treasury Economic Model (ITEM) Club published its forecasts for the economy. The club is a group of economists who pool their knowledge to prepare quarterly forecasts using the Treasury's computer forecasting model. Club members represent a cross-section of publicly and privately owned industry, banking, finance and public administration. These forecasts are not designed to support any particular theory or to try to persuade the government to make any particular change of policy.

The summary of their conclusions was that the Conservative government's monetary policies would not bring inflation back into single figures (where it was just before they took office) before 1983; that, by then, 3 million people would be unemployed, and output would have fallen 8 per cent from its 1979 peak; that the balance of payments current account deficit would remain persistently over £3 billion a year; that the Public Sector Borrowing Requirement would rise again from the target £8.25 billion in 1980 to £11.5 billion in 1981, because of increased unemployment and social security expenditure; and that one-sixth of manufacturing industry would be destroyed as a result of government policies. Only the financial sector of the economy would benefit from these changes, as interest rates would fall only slowly, and sterling would keep much of its strength.

The ITEM Club's report simply quantified the sort of forecasts that had been made by industrialists and economists throughout the first half of 1980. The report addressed itself not to the slump, which was well under way when it was published, but to the 'recovery' anticipated by the Conservative government:[13]

It now seems that it will be very late and very small with the famous 'supply side' of the economy devastated over the next couple of years by de-industrialisation, mass unemployment and low investment. This should come as no surprise. Britain has a mixed economy. To this the government has applied its pure competition theories. Monetary policy works through the market. In so far as the policy succeeds, it does so by squeezing output, increasing unemployment and so eventually choking off inflation, primarily in the open competition fractions of the economy. That success further reduces the limited area in which the policy operates, raising its cost and reducing its impact.

ITEM forecasted that inflation would still be running at about 11.5 per cent in the second half of 1982, having been around 15 per cent in 1981:[14]

The price of this limited success in the fight against inflation is a terrible slump. National output is expected to fall 3½ per cent in 1980, 5 per cent in 1981, and then to remain virtually unchanged in 1982: a cumulative decline of 8¼ per cent from the modest 1979 peak over the three years to 1982. Since North Sea Oil output is expected to rise steadily over this period, the on-shore slump in output is even greater. 1982 is expected to be 10 per cent down on 1979 and 4½ per cent down on the dreadful year of 1975. Manufacturing industry does even worse — 16½ per cent down on 1979 and 13 per cent down on 1975.

The forecast stated unequivocally that unemployment would double in three years and stand at 3 million by the end of 1982. Earnings would fall as industry cut back production, and overtime and bonus payments were reduced. The report suggested that earnings would be about 2 per cent below the rate of inflation in 1980-1, and 2.5 per cent below it in 1981-2:[15]

Real disposable incomes fall slightly throughout the economy over the next two years even for those in work. This fall is greatest in the public sector, but the greatest burden for the slump is borne by the extra million and a half unemployed.

The real value of personal incomes would fall by 4.25 per cent in 1981 and another 2 per cent in 1982, the report predicted.

For private industry, the effects of policy were expected to be drastic. Private investment would be down by 14.25 per cent in 1981. The ITEM report emphasised that monetary policy would only work by attacking the competitive sector of the market, and that hence, when government wielded the monetarist sword, 'with each blow both industrial friend and inflationary foe are felled.'[16] Conservatives would argue that policies squeeze the least efficient out of business; yet the one-sixth of manufacturing industry ITEM forecasted as likely to be destroyed by monetarist measures is a very large proportion to sacrifice in three years.

Here again, the burden of austerity is likely to be unevenly shared. Firms with low profits will close down, but firms like Ford, who made a £347 million profit after tax in 1979, will use the opportunity of the recession to press forward with automation and redundancies, despite high interest rates and low demand. The government shows no signs of recognising the 'Ricardo phenomenon' — that monetary policy simply accelerates the trend towards more profitable industries saving labour costs through new technology, while making no increase in output. Hence, unemployment is fed from two sources — from de-industrialisation on the one hand, and from technological change on the other.

It is difficult to predict beyond 1982, but the ITEM report suggests that trade unions in the industrial sector will succeed in holding real wage reductions to about 2 to 2.5 per cent in the next three years. This would mean that government hopes of lower wages would be confined to the non-industrial sector, and mainly to services. Any improvement in the employment situation would thus rely on low-productivity, low-wage jobs, which would have less effect on output. The problem of growth would remain unsolved; its social manifestations would be alarmingly emphasised. In the final part of this book I shall examine social policy in relation to this problem.

Part 3

6 Social policy 1964-70

(i) Poverty and the Labour government

In 1980, the dominant issue of economic and social policy is unemployment. Out of this issue arises a growing confrontation about the causes of and remedies for a figure of over 2 million unemployed. Employers and the Conservative government blame unions for excessive wages and maldistribution of labour; trade unions accuse employers and government of excessive cuts in the workforce of both public and private sectors. The government has reduced unemployment benefit, and is considering further reductions; claimants' organisations argue that benefits were already inadequate.

I have argued that this issue has emerged through the 'Ricardo phenomenon' of increased productivity and static output. However, to understand the conflict over social policy, we need to trace the history of the state's response to the social consequences of this phenomenon. This requires consideration of the policies of the Labour government in the 1960s. Problems about the state's role in the relief of poverty, which had ceased to be an issue in the previous fifteen years, began to re-emerge in this period. The way in which the Labour government handled these questions influenced the shape of policies for the next decade.

For all its rhetoric about neglected social services, Labour's main priority in 1964 was industrial. The new government's approach was summed up in two sentences from the National Plan of 1965:[1]

The task of correcting the balance of payments, and achieving the surplus necessary to repay our debts, while at the same time fostering the rapid growth of the economy, is the central challenge. We

must succeed if we are to achieve all our objectives of social justice
and welfare, . . . and of a full life for all in a pleasant environment.

Labour came to power with certain specific social policy proposals on
Comprehensive education, rents and prescription charges; but it had no
radical social philosophy with which to tackle the structural problems
of poverty and unemployment that emerged in the late 1960s.

In social security, its main priority was the elderly, who were seen
as an important electoral target group. As a secondary aim, it wanted
to adapt social security provision so as to smooth the path of the
'shakeout' of labour from industry. With hindsight, it is clear that the
really important issues of the period were low-income families, and the
beginning of technological unemployment. Labour had no policies
for these problems.

Hence the government responded in hasty and expedient ways to
issues as they arose, without planning or foresight. Yet many of these
ad hoc solutions formed the basis of later policies and administrative
structures in the 1970s. For instance, Labour wanted to abolish
National Assistance, but ended up by using it as the basis of an expanded system of means-tested benefits. The consequences of that
decision are still being felt in our income maintenance schemes today.

Another important feature of the period was that the trade union
movement took little interest in social policy. Embroiled in their
negotiations over prices and incomes, and in the intricacies of
productivity-dealing, trade unionists left issues of poverty and other
social problems to newly founded middle-class pressure groups. These
tended to present questions of social policy in highly technical terms,
which isolated them from questions about economic structure. Hence
the political economy of social welfare became obscured at a time when
crucial issues should have been emerging, and the working class was
largely cut off from the debate about social policy for the next decade.

In this chapter, I shall deal mainly with issues of social security
provision during this era. In the next chapter I shall look more generally
at the social services.

(ii) Labour in opposition

During its years in opposition, the Labour Party criticised the Conservatives for neglecting the social services. It promised to improve

services generally, and social security in particular, when it took office. As we shall see in this chapter, these promises were not fulfilled, and alternative strategies were developed as short-term expedients. More ambitious plans were postponed, waiting on the day when technological progress would produce economic growth – the day which never came.

In the early 1960s, a number of Labour Party leaders committed themselves to statements about the high priority that would be given to social service expenditure by the next Labour government. Anthony Crosland wrote in 1962 that[2]

A Socialist is identified as one who wishes to give this an exceptional priority over other claims on resources. . . . This represents the major difference between a Socialist and a Conservative. . . . We shall not put matters right unless we increase the proportion of the national income devoted to social purposes.

Douglas Jay wrote that 'Government and local authority expenditure . . . has always been too low: it is too low today and ought to be increased . . . the assault on poverty and inequality through redistribution must remain the prime purpose for a long time ahead.'[3] Richard Crossman told the Party Conference in 1960 that Labour's social security reforms would not be confined to a new superannuation scheme for the elderly; they would seek to abolish National Assistance for all claimant groups by raising National Insurance benefits. The Labour Party document 'New Frontiers for Social Security' (1963) announced that its plans would 'signalise the abolition of poverty by creating a new Ministry to administer our new system of social security.'[4]

At this time, the debate about poverty focused mainly on the elderly. The Labour Party accused the Conservatives of allowing the state pensions scheme to fall into neglect by allowing it to become a limited service for supplementing occupational pensions. This meant that higher numbers of low-paid workers and their wives, who would never qualify for occupational schemes, were being forced onto National Assistance. Richard Crossman told the 1960 Labour Conference that this was[5]

part of Tory policy: they are quite deliberately keeping the rate of benefit at a point where you are compelled to go to National

Assistance in order to live. I have only to quote you the figures;
82,000 more pensions have had to go to National Assistance this
year than last.

The party had published its plans for 'National Superannuation:
Labour's Policy for Security in Old Age' in 1957. It was a comprehensive earnings-related scheme, which was the main plank of Labour's
social programme up to the election of 1964, and represented a complete departure from the Beveridge scheme of flat-rate benefits. The
aim was to take the great majority of elderly claimants off National
Assistance, but this was a long-term strategy, and would not take
immediate effect. Accordingly a short-term plan was developed. Pensions would be raised immediately and an 'income guarantee' would
be introduced. This was intended to be a more generous supplement
to the existing pensions scheme than National Assistance. It would
provide a sliding scale of benefit to needier claimants, according to
a far briefer and simpler test of income, and was intended to reduce
stigma and increase willingness to claim. The scales would be raised
over a period of seven years, removing an increasing proportion of
the elderly from National Assistance during this time, and providing
a transition from the old pensions scheme to the new, earnings-related
one.

Labour's plans were given further impetus by research published in
1962. Cole and Utting suggested that at least 500,000 (and probably
as many as 700,000) old people who would be eligible for National
Assistance were not applying for it.[6] This confirmed Labour's criticisms
of the fear of stigma attached to National Assistance by the elderly.
Not only were too many old people having to claim assistance; many
others were too proud (or too unaware of their entitlement) to do so.

Accordingly, Labour's manifesto of 1964 placed considerable
emphasis on pensions and the 'income guarantee', as part of a general
strategy of earnings-related benefits: 'Social security benefits . . . have
been allowed to fall below minimum levels of human need. Consequently one in four of National Insurance pensioners are today depend-
ing upon means-tested National Assistance benefits. Labour will re-
construct our social security system.' After outlining plans for earnings-
related sickness and unemployment benefits as well as pensions, and
for linking all National Insurance benefits to average wages, the manifesto specifically pledged that the introduction of the income guarantee
was urgent and unconditional:[7]

Labour recognises that the nation cannot have first-rate social security on the cheap. For . . . [this] reason we stress that, with the exception of the early introduction of the Income Guarantee, the key factor in determining the speed at which new and better levels of benefit can be introduced, will be the rate at which the British economy can advance.

(iii) Labour's social priorities

As promised, the new government did raise pensions and introduce earnings-related schemes for unemployment and sickness on taking office. However, the increase in the rates of National Insurance benefits was expensive, and took a large share of the allocation for social services which Labour had made in its pre-election planning. It cost £285 million, and was based on plans for a growth rate of 4 per cent in the economy as a whole (see Chapter 3). In fact, growth was much slower than this. Consequently, both the superannuation scheme and the income guarantee were shelved.

Indeed, when Labour's National Plan was published in 1965, critics were not slow to draw attention to the low priority given to social service expenditure. In a Fabian tract published in 1966, Abel-Smith castigated the government for its lack of socialist principles:[8]

How does the distribution of resources for the six years 1958 to 1964 compare with that planned for the six years 1964 to 1970?. . . . The calculation shows that the public services (current) and housing increased by 34.5 per cent in constant prices between 1958 and 1964 and are planned to increase by only 28 per cent between 1964 and 1970. Thus the absolute rate of growth was greater in the six years preceding 1964 than in the six years planned from 1964 onwards.

Abel-Smith pointed out that in housing, health (excepting the abolition of prescription charges) and education, Labour planned for less expansion than the Tories had achieved; in social security, Labour's allowance for increase was lower than its planned growth for wages. He contrasted the high principle of Labour leaders when out of office with the National Plan's subjugation of social expenditure to aims of economic policy. This was certainly a fair criticism; for instance, earnings-related, short-term benefits (sickness and unemployment) had been given priority over the superannuation scheme and income guarantee, partly because they cost little, but also because they eased the way for the 'shakeout' of labour and reflationary policies.

Abel-Smith and Townsend also added to evidence of need for an improved superannuation scheme in their study *The Poor and the Poorest*, published in 1965. They, too, found evidence of 0.75 million elderly people who did not claim National Assistance, in spite of incomes below the poverty line — a finding that was confirmed by the official survey of the problem set up by the new government. Abel-Smith and Townsend's other findings, about poverty among the working population, will be discussed in section (v) of this chapter.

Short-term unemployment and sickness benefits hardly represented a revolutionary change; they were self-financing in the long run, out of increased contributions, and cost only £60 million in their first year. The superannuation scheme and income guarantee were postponed — the latter despite the specific pledge to introduce it 'without delay'. Webb considers that as well as the Labour government's primary concern with its economic policies, and particularly its obsession with the balance of payments, administrative considerations played an important part in the failure of the income guarantee.[9] In opposition, Labour had not even decided how rents, the main component of need, would be calculated. Nor had policies about the groups still left on National Assistance been spelled out. These uncertainties made the scheme vulnerable to fatal delays by civil servants. It also required co-ordination between a number of government departments, including the Inland Revenue, which was particularly reluctant to co-operate; the new ministers involved were inexperienced, and Douglas Houghton's role as 'overlord' in social security questions was inadequate to the task, if not actually unhelpful.

In the event, changes in short-term benefits made by Labour had a limited life-span; the Conservatives abolished earnings-related supplements in 1980. But the failure to introduce the income guarantee had more far-reaching consequences. National Assistance was 're-formed', but it was abolished in name only. The changes made under Labour consolidated its functions and established the foundations on which the 'mass role' of the 1980s was built. Supplementary benefits were to become proportionately the largest means-tested system in Western Europe.

(iv) The creation of the Supplementary Benefits Commission

National Assistance had been set up in 1948 to give 'assistance subject to means test ... administered with sympathetic justice and discretion, taking full account of individual circumstances' to those who 'can never contribute at all or who fall through the meshes of any insurance scheme.'[10] Although Douglas Houghton claimed in the House of Commons in 1964 that there were only 'three institutions in Britain about which no hard word can be said in this House – the Crown, the Church, and the National Assistance Board,' and that the Board's staff equipped them to be 'the citizens' friend',[11] criticisms of its work had been growing. When the income guarantee scheme was abandoned, attention turned to how a more acceptable form of means-tested public assistance could be given to the rising number of claimants who still required it. Attention was focused chiefly on the needs of the elderly, who formed 62 per cent of all claimants.

Accordingly, in 1966, the Ministry of Social Security Act established the Supplementary Benefits Commission. The new Act aimed at establishing 'rights' to benefit, reducing stigma, widening publicity, and making the assistance scheme more understandable and predictable – all in an attempt to improve the image of a means-tested system. The changes were partly in the regulations themselves, and partly in the administration. The rate of benefits was increased; the limits on eligibility from income and capital were raised and simplified; a standard addition to weekly rates for long-term claimants replaced occasional discretionary additions. None of these changes was structural, and all could have been made within the framework of National Assistance. But the administrative changes, aimed at reducing stigma and forestalling criticisms about low take-up, required a new structure. Supplementary benefits were to be part of the system administered by the new ministry, which was an amalgamation of the old Ministry of Pensions and National Insurance, and the National Assistance Board. The many separate offices of the two agencies were to be merged into a few large district offices, from which both would be organised. Although the rules governing eligibility and the calculation of entitlement of the two schemes remained as entirely different as ever (supplementary benefits still required as detailed an assessment of the claimant's resources and requirements), the merging of the offices made it look as if the new benefits were part of the same overall system as National Insurance. In addition, the elderly were to receive their weekly supplementary pensions at the post office in the same order book as their pensions.

In the event, an extra 356,000 elderly people claimed assistance between October and December 1966, and the attempt to reduce stigma seemed to have succeeded. However, Atkinson's research suggested that 'between half and two-thirds of the increase between December 1965 and December 1968 ... can be attributed to the more generous assistance scale.'[12] He argued that a similar increase would have occurred under National Assistance. If the changes achieved anything, it was rather in the direction of down-grading the status of National Insurance benefits. Increasingly since 1966 when social security is discussed, members of the general public assume that this means supplementary benefit — indeed the two terms have become virtually synonymous. By merging the main Beveridge scheme with the residuum of the Poor Law, which he intended to wither away, Labour gave a spurious respectability to the means-tested system, while heavily contaminating the one based on contributions. Labour, pledged to abolish National Assistance, instead created in supplementary benefits a scheme based entirely on Poor Law principles which has been expanding ever since.

Furthermore, the new scheme came into existence precisely at the moment when the productive workforce began to decline, and structural unemployment started to be a feature of the economy. Thus the new short-term earnings-related unemployment benefits, which lasted only six months from the date of first claim, were inadequate for the problem that emerged. By 1968, there were 220,000 unemployed claimants of supplementary benefits; by 1971 there were 387,000. Taken together with the steady increase in single parents claiming, this soon emerged as the chief source of new claims.

Yet the new regulations and administrative systems had been designed to meet the needs of elderly, long-term claimants. The reform of National Assistance was a substitute for the income guarantee, and reflected Labour's preoccupation with pensions and pensioners. The rules of supplementary benefits still applied a wage stop to unemployed claimants. This meant that benefits were held down to a level below their requirements, calculated from their previous earnings. It applied particularly to unemployed claimants with large families, and kept the children of such families below the poverty line. In 1970, 33,000 claimants (14 per cent of unemployed beneficiaries) had their benefits reduced by wage stop. Second, even if an unemployed claimant was on supplementary benefit for over two years, he did not qualify for the long-term rate of benefit, which was the main respect in which the new scheme was more generous than the old. Third, the administrative changes favoured the elderly, and disadvantaged younger claimants. For pensioners, order books, fewer official visits, and an appointment system for office interviews introduced in the late 1960s, were all improvements. For young families on the breadline — whose claims were more often for shorter periods, whose requirements were frequently changing, and who ran into occasional crises over large fuel bills, clothing needs, debts on rent payments — all these administrative changes introduced an unresponsive rigidity into the system. For these neediest claimants, National Assistance — with its network of little local offices, paying cash weekly over the counter, and its reliance on visiting officers with discretion to meet extra needs — was actually a better system.

Paradoxically, also, the emphasis on rights to supplementary benefits, and the increase in publicity, had the effect of increasing consciousness in officials and politicians of the dangers of abuse. Under National Assistance, the problem of fraud had constantly been played down. Successive annual reports denied that abuse occurred on any significant scale, and the very nature of a small local service, with much face-to-face contact, probably created an atmosphere of familiarity, if not mutual respect. Supplementary benefits — concentrated into large district office blocks, employing more and more clerical staff who assessed claimants' needs on paper, rather than in person — was a far more anonymous system. As claims from single parents and the unemployed increased, so did suspicion and hostility between staff and claimants. In 1969 we saw the creation of the first Claimants Union — groups of mainly young people, highly critical of the principles and methods of supplementary benefits, organised to discredit the system, and maximise discretionary claims.

These trends were reflected in political attitudes. Between 1964 and 1966 there were considerable criticisms of the way National Assistance was administered, and sympathy for younger claimants as well as the elderly. A Conservative MP, Mr Curran, asked the Labour government 'to review the wages stop so as not to penalise the man with a large family and to recognise that, as we are doing it now, we are clamping down on the loafer at the expense of his children.' He thought it better 'to put up with a certain amount of cheating and fiddling rather than penalise the man with a large family.'[13] Yet by

1968, when unemployment figures were double those of 1964, Labour MPs were raising questions about 'scroungers' and 'layabouts' on supplementary benefits, and their concern was echoed with doubled intensity by Conservatives. As a result of this outcry, the Supplementary Benefits Commission introduced the 'four week rule', under which an able-bodied single claimant under the age of forty-five could be refused further payments if he had not found himself another job in this period. In some areas the single unemployed were refused payment altogether, and told to move elsewhere in search of work. Hence the notion of a 'right' to supplementary benefit provoked a backlash, and accusations of 'abuse', especially as unemployment figures rose.

(v) Family poverty

Abel-Smith and Townsend are credited with having 'rediscovered poverty' in the researches that led to their publication *The Poor and the Poorest* (1965), mainly because they drew attention to the continued existence of large numbers of poor families with an employed bread-winner. Family poverty had not been a political issue since the 1940s. The value of tax allowances for children (which in any case did not benefit the poorest families as much as the better off, and in some cases did not benefit them at all) had been declining with inflation over the previous twenty years; so had the value of family allowances (as child benefits were then called). Abel-Smith and Townsend showed that in 1960 two-fifths of those living in poverty by their criteria (National Assistance scales plus 40 per cent) were in households that were primarily dependent on earnings. These families contained 2.25 million children, of whom 650,000 were in households where the income was actually below the National Assistance scales.[14]

The history of policy on family poverty under the Labour government of 1964 to 1979 was a complex and tangled one, partly because the leaders of the Child Poverty Action Group (CPAG, which came into existence at the time Able-Smith and Townsend's study was published) had been advisers to the Labour Party's policy group in their years in opposition. In spite of the stir caused by the 'rediscovery of poverty', the government postponed action on family allowances, the CPAG's main target, until 1967. Then it raised them by 35p per child, but at the same time increased the charges for school dinners and welfare milk by 50 per cent. Six months later, it raised family allowances by another 15p, but simultaneously adjusted child tax allowances so as to 'claw back' most of this increase from taxpaying parents. The tax increases came into effect before the small increase in family allowances, and were very unpopular.

During this period, the CPAG achieved a great deal of publicity, and some influence, but its tactics were questionable. It changed its recommendations on policy reform on several occasions, and its publications tended to be academic and somewhat technical. 'Clawback' was one of its proposals; it subsequently castigated the government and itself for not explaining its virtues to the public.[15] Since CPAG itself later found an esoteric drawback about 'clawback', and advocated a return to a 'fully universal' benefit,[16] the public perhaps had some reason to be mystified.

The CPAG was right to emphasise the importance of family allowances; indeed it was more right than its often obscure arguments suggested. Family allowances were the only method of paying a state income to people in full-time work that existed in the mid-1960s. Their own researches showed that poverty persisted among wage-earners. With hindsight it can be seen that what their campaigns should have emphasised was the growing need for universal benefits for the employed as well as for the unemployed. As technological unemployment began to appear, and productivity to rise, what was needed was a policy for income maintenance based on sharing work and leisure, and paying the benefits of new technology to all, in the form of a guaranteed weekly income. Family allowances were both an accepted (though research suggested a not very popular)[17] means of doing this, and a direct way of helping the poorest families. Unfortunately, they also raised issues about population and child care over which the British were notoriously bigoted, and governments absurdly nervous. The emotive question of children living in poverty cut both ways: it conjured up spectres of feckless parents as well as images of deprived children. The real issue should have been the future of income maintenance policy for the employed, and not simply the question of child benefits and allowances.

In the event, the CPAG was able to claim that its campaigns had gained some £50 million for poor families under the Labour government; but it had also to acknowledge that its increasingly bitter technical wrangles with the government might have played some part in Labour's election failure in 1970.[18] Furthermore, both the Labour government and their Conservative successors were able to use evidence about family poverty in support of means-tested benefits, claiming that the CPAG were pressing them to 'do something about child poverty' at a time when economic necessities would not permit increases in universal allowances. Thus, for instance, David Ennals, then Minister of State for Social Security, claimed, with injured innocence, in 1970 that 'There are now some 600,000 more people (old people, widows, the sick, unemployed, deserted wives, etc.) drawing supplementary benefits than received national assistance — yet Child Poverty Action Group condemns us for this achievement. You just can't win.'[19]

Indeed, as early as 1966, Labour had introduced a means-tested rate rebate scheme, from which families of wage-earners could benefit. However, only about two-thirds of all eligible claimants came forward to apply for this new assistance, and only about 10 per cent of eligible wage-earners with families applied.[20] Yet this evidence of stigma and inefficiency did not discredit the scheme; it served as a model for the plethora of new selective benefits which followed under the Conservatives. Neither government wanted to tackle family poverty; both were forced to do something about it because incomes did not increase in line with productivity, or even with the modest levels of growth achieved. Selective supplementation of low wages was therefore the expedient solution adopted. I shall return to this theme in the next chapter.

(vi) Positive discrimination

While Labour ministers were becoming (contrary to their election pledges) reluctant selectivists, some kind of intellectual framework had to be hurriedly constructed to justify this conversion to the virtues of the means test. The nearest approximation was to be found in the philosophy of 'positive discrimination'. This expression was enshrined in the works of Professor Titmuss, who wrote, in 1968:[21]

The challenge that faces us is not the choice between universalist and selective social services. The real challenge resides in this question: what particular infrastructure of universalist services is needed in order to provide a framework of values and opportunity bases within and around which can be developed socially acceptable selective services aiming to discriminate positively, with the minimum risk of stigma, in favour of those whose needs are greatest.

This notion had the advantage of providing an inexhaustible source of creative-sounding rhetoric, liberally drawn upon by government spokesmen. It also could be linked with various well-intentioned programmes sponsored by the Kennedy and Johnson administrations in the United States.

The main projects sponsored under this banner were the Educational Priority Areas (in response to the Plowden Report of 1966), the Urban Programme and, in 1969, the Community Development Projects. The purpose of all of them was to provide extra resources for areas of special and multiple social need, but to reduce stigma by concentrating on deprived areas rather than deprived individuals. Attempts were also to be made to co-ordinate the work of welfare agencies, and to promote participation of ordinary citizens in the provision of services. In spite of these high aims, the expenditure on the projects was minimal. Michael Meacher showed that by 1972-3, the Urban Programme constituted 0.05 per cent of total public expenditure, and 0.1 per cent of social services expenditure; the Community Development Projects cost only a small fraction of the Urban Programme. The Educational Priority Areas attracted 1 per cent of the total educational budget for improvement and replacement of schools, and a further small sum on increments to teachers' salaries.[22]

Meacher went on to suggest that 'there is a marked discrepancy of interest in the Positive Discrimination Programmes between field-work activists, who want to redistribute power and opportunity, and governments, who want to show maximum concern at minimum costs in ways that cannot fundamentally alter society.'[23] As Barnes pointed out, in the same publication, the programmes were ambiguous: they did not make it clear whether they were intended to take people out of poverty, or to take poverty out of people.[24] They implied that in very poor areas people had desperate and unusual needs, and that many factors interacted with and caused each other, making everything worse for everybody. But by spending so little to put this right, they suggested it was the people themselves who had to change, or be changed. And they paved the way for Conservative theories, based on the notion of a demoralising 'culture of poverty' — 'the cycle of deprivation', which will be discussed in the next chapter.

(vii) The personal social services: the Seebohm Report

The only thoroughgoing reform that Labour carried out was of the personal social services, at that time a small sector of the state's welfare provision. This had been a modest part of Labour's planning since the late 1950s, but in its implementation the emphasis of the changes altered subtly, and this affected the way the social services departments later developed.

The ideas behind the notion of a unified local authority Personal Social Services Department could be traced to attempts to reform the provision for juvenile delinquents. An influential group of Labour Party spokesmen studied experiments, particularly in Oxfordshire, to divert delinquents from the approved schools, and where possible from the courts, by using the facilities of the Children's Department. The thinking that led to these initiatives was reflected in the Labour Party's document 'Crime − A Challenge to Us All' (the Longford Report) which called for a 'family service' to provide counselling for the parents of delinquent children, and community-based services for those who had to be removed from home.[25] The new government published two White Papers on delinquency, and set up the Seebohm Committee, which reported in 1968, recommending the amalgamation of the Children's Departments, Welfare Departments (which gave residential and domiciliary care to the elderly) and mental health services. This was in line with the Longford Report's proposals, but the scope of the new departments was to be far wider. Instead of being a family service, focused mainly on the needs of children and young people, the new department was to be responsible for the whole range of domiciliary and residential services offered by local authorities to deprived, handicapped or deviant individuals.

The Seebohm Report, which had recommended the creation of the social services departments, argued that a large, unified agency was necessary in order to attract more resources, to plan services more appropriately and to take an overview of the needs of the community. The new departments were intended to take their place alongside the major social services. This was in line with the prevalent philosophy of the late 1960s − that it was possible to provide extra help selectively, without excessive stigma, and that this should be given priority over extensions of universal services. Indeed, the personal social services were to grow more rapidly than any other social agency in the first half of the 1970s, and unification undoubtedly paved the way for this expansion. However, the Seebohm Report did not anticipate the problems that this entailed. With the creation of a large new department, providing a range of benefits and services for all the most disadvantaged citizens, there developed a strong tendency for this to be the 'dustbin' for the other agencies. As they referred on all their problem cases to the social services departments, a new category of stigmatised recipients of state assistance came into being. Referring on to social workers became an alternative to providing an appropriate service for the neediest and most demanding clients of the major social agencies. This will be discussed more fully in the next two chapters.

(viii) Conclusion

The Labour government came to power with certain clear-cut social policies, but with no comprehensive social philosophy with which to tackle the many issues which were raised by the economic changes that took place between 1964 and 1970. Its ideas on social security — to convert National Insurance into an earnings-related scheme — were intended to bring the Beveridge Welfare State in line with an affluent consumer society, and to smooth the path of rapid economic growth based on new technology. It had no ready-made answers to the problems of structural unemployment and family poverty which quickly emerged, and the failure of its economic policies destroyed its will to promote social change. The Crossman diaries reveal the Labour ministers who made such high promises when in opposition squabbling among themselves for a share of the very low allocation made to social services, and indicate the dearth of any overall strategy for decisions about social priorities.

The result was that the government was hurried into a number of important decisions which were taken without proper planning or consideration of the long-term consequences. The most crucial of these concerned the extension of means-tested benefits. Under the Conservatives, selectivism was carried several stages further, as we shall see in the next chapter. The failure of the Labour government to improve the effectiveness of universal benefits in the struggle against poverty, amongst the employed and the unemployed, proved irreversible in the 1970s.

7 Social policy 1970-9

The two major themes of British social policy in the 1970s were the rapid expansion of social services expenditure, and attempts, from 1975 onwards, to control this expansion. These attempts (since replaced by more abrasive Conservative measures) were made from fear of allowing social services to use scarce resources that could have been employed in productive industry, and thus stultifying economic growth. During the later 1970s, the notion that social services were competing for resources with productive industry gained ground, and strongly influenced policy.

In fact, as I shall show, the expansion of the social services was to a great extent a response to the social consequences of the 'Ricardo phenomenon'. During the Heath government's attempt to reduce unemployment, it consisted largely of an increase in (mainly low-wage) employment in the social services. After 1975, such expansion as took place was largely in transfer payments − money transferred from the employed workforce to non-employed people. In other words, both kinds of expansion were reactions to the twin phenomena of increased unemployment and higher productivity in industry. They were provided out of the resources saved by a more automated productive industry (reduced labour costs) and out of the higher earnings of remaining workers. However, after the crisis over oil prices, and after the Labour government had abandoned the aim of full employment, and begun to pursue a modified form of monetarism, jobs in the social services were cut. Transfer payments went on growing with increased unemployment.

Expenditure on social services increased in similar proportions in all the other European countries, and in the United States and Japan, during this period. However, in Britain there was a particular emphasis on selective benefits, especially for those of working age. Because technological unemployment was combined with low rates of growth, Britain chose the cheapest possible method of expanding services to meet the needs created by the 'Ricardo phenomenon' – means-tested benefits and services. Resentment against state beneficiaries increased in line with the growth of selective benefits.

(i) The expansion of the social services

The proportion of GDP devoted to the social services in Britain grew at an accelerating rate between the early 1950s and the mid-1970s. From 1975 onwards it started to decline. This is shown in the figures given in Table 7.1.[1]

Table 7.1

	1951	1961	1968	1971	1975	1978
Total expenditure on social services (including housing) as a percentage of GDP at market prices	11.5	15.6	19.5	19.6	25.6	24.1

This expansion in social services expenditure as a proportion of GDP was paralleled in every Western industrialised country. In all the Organization for Economic Co-operation and Development (OECD) nations, public spending on social services grew more rapidly than the national income between the early 1960s and the mid-1970s.[2] Britain's increase in social services expenditure was average for the OECD in this period, taking account of its rate of economic growth. Thus, in 1975, Britain's proportion of GDP devoted to social services was still considerably lower than France's, Germany's and Sweden's; slightly lower than Canada's and Italy's; and slightly higher than that of the United States.

The increase in social services expenditure can usefully be divided between resource spending and transfers. Resource spending is expenditure on labour, energy, buildings and other goods. Transfers are payments by the state to its beneficiaries, mainly through social security, but also through such items as subsidies on housing and food, and various rebates. Between 1968 and 1975 resource spending in the social services grew slightly more rapidly than transfer spending in Britain; from 1975 onwards, resource spending was cut back, and the expansion that took place was in transfer spending (see Table 7.2).[3]

Table 7.2

	1968	1971	1975	1978
Resource spending in social services (including housing) (£m., at 1975 prices)	8,892	9,515	14,169	12,857
Index of resource spending	62.8	67.2	100.0	90.7
Transfer spending in social services (including housing) (£m., at 1975 prices)	9,333	9,533	13,954	15,085
Index of transfer spending	66.9	68.3	100.0	108.1

The figures in Table 7.2 show that there was a much more rapid increase in both resource and transfer spending between 1971 and 1975 than there had been during the previous four years. Both resource and transfer spending increased by nearly 50 per cent between 1971 and 1975 (i.e. during the Heath government, and the first year of the subsequent Labour government). It is worth looking in more detail at this period of very rapid expansion of social services expenditure.

Figure 7.1 provides an analysis of the growth of total spending on the various social services during these four years, and shows how the cuts in social services expenditure were distributed between the services between 1975 and 1978.[4] From these figures it can be seen that spending on housing increased most rapidly between 1971 and 1975 — by over 100 per cent in all. Spending on the personal social services increased by an even larger percentage. Spending on education and the National Health Service, though it increased rather less rapidly, also grew fairly evenly throughout this period. The increase in social security spending was more modest — under 25 per cent in four years.

However, when we compare the rate of increase in spending on capital projects and on wages during the same period, it becomes clear that there were three distinct phases in the expansion and the cuts. Between 1971 and 1973, capital programmes were undertaken

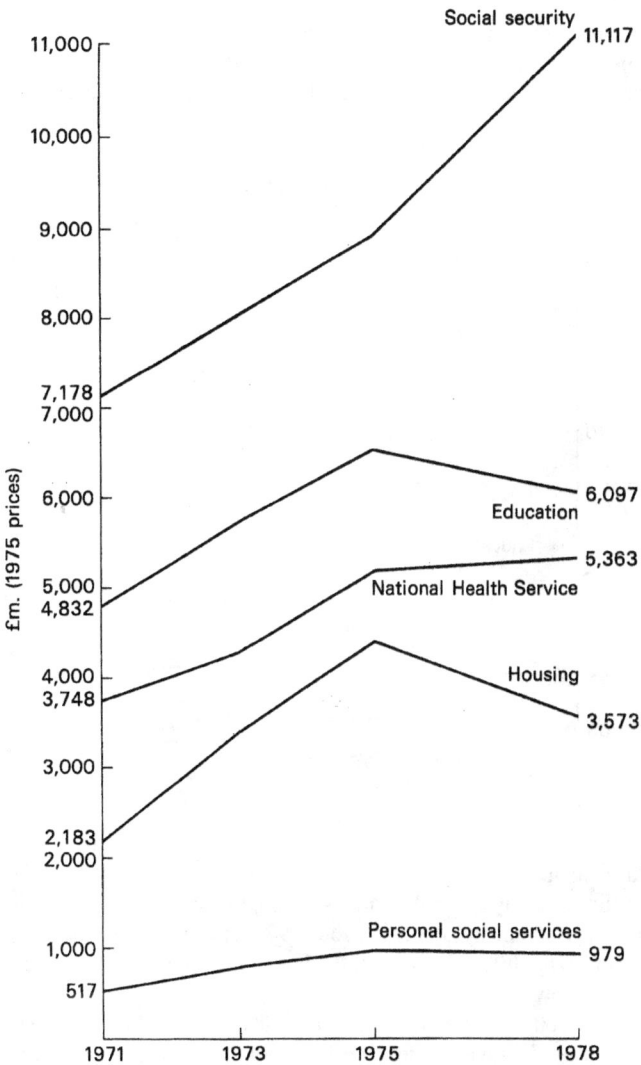

Figure 7.1 Total government expenditure on social services

on quite an ambitious scale (see Figure 7.2) particularly the building of schools, hospitals, council houses and residential facilities in the personal social services. From 1973 onwards, building programmes (except those for council houses) were cut back. However, there was a compensatory expansion of employment in the social services. Wage bills rose rapidly between 1973 and 1975 (see Figure 7.3), particularly in health, education and the personal social services, as more ancillary staff were taken on, and the administration of the health service was reorganised. This expansion of employment in the social services

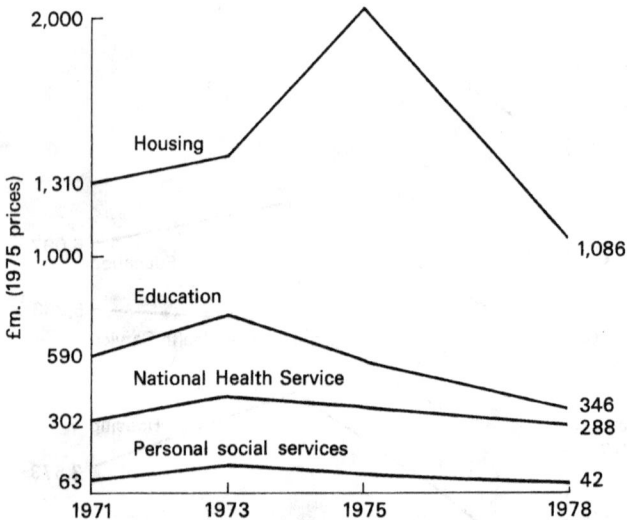

Figure 7.2 Capital expenditure in the social services

coincided with the Heath government's attempts at Keynesian reflation of the economy through public spending; it was a direct response to high rates of unemployment. From 1975 onwards, this expansion ceased, and wage bills fell slightly; the building programme in housing was also savagely cut.[5]

As both capital programmes and wage bills were cut between 1975 and 1978, transfer spending increased. Figure 7.4 indicates the growth in transfer spending in the three main services through which it occurs.[6]

Thus under the Labour government, from 1975 onwards, there was a considerable attempt to reduce expenditure in the social services, through cutting back capital programmes, and through reductions in total wage payments. But because of the increase in poverty and

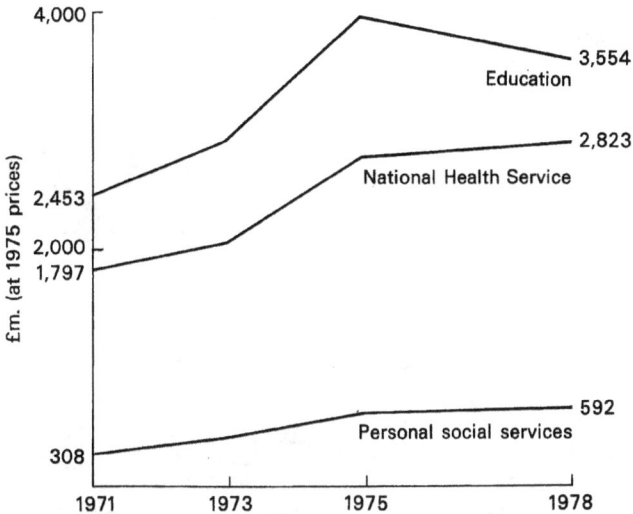

Figure 7.3 Expenditure on wages and salaries in the social services

unemployment that was taking place, transfer payments expanded slightly. Whereas increases in capital expenditure and employment in the social services before 1975 were planned and intended by government, from 1975 onwards the intention was to save money wherever possible; increased transfer spending was largely unplanned, and was a direct effect of the failure of the productive economy to distribute adequate incomes to a large proportion of the population.

Between 1975 and 1978, total government spending on the social services (including housing) declined from 25.6 per cent to 24.1 per cent of GDP. But total transfer spending increased from 13.4 to 13.5 per cent of GDP.

(ii) Causes and consequences of the expansion of the social services

There were several non-economic and non-political reasons why expenditure on the social services increased in the 1960s and 1970s. The most obvious of these was demographic. Between 1941 and 1971 the total population of the UK grew by 13.5 per cent; but the population below 16 years of age grew by 28.9 per cent; and the population

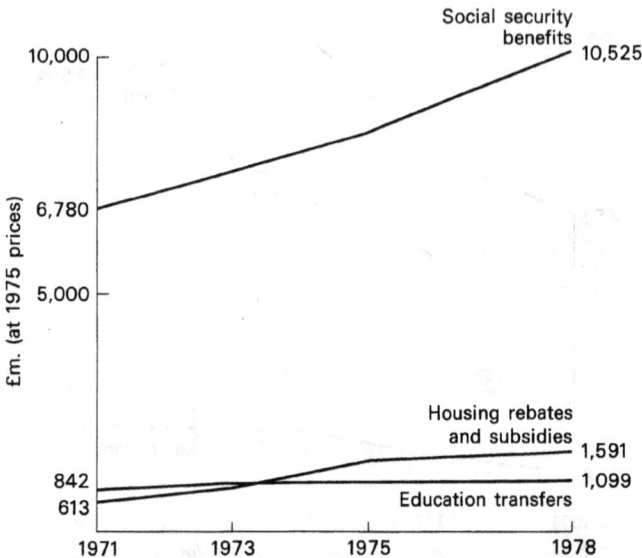

Figure 7.4   Transfer spending in the social services

over retirement age grew by 37.4 per cent. Since these two groups
(children and the elderly) are the most extensive and expensive consumers of social services, this change in the balance of the British
population made a major contribution to increased social services
expenditure.

Another factor in rising costs of these services might be classed
as technological. While automation was reducing labour costs in productive industry, the social services could not match these improvements in productivity. The social services are by their nature labour
intensive, and up to now new technology has not affected their work.
Consequently, there was a rise in the relative costs of social services
compared with productive industry (the relative price effect). The
same phenomenon occurred in all the other OECD countries.[7]

However, as we have seen in the last section, the main reason why
expenditure grew so rapidly between 1971 and 1975 was the economic
situation in Britain, and governments' response to it. It was this
response that gave rise to a number of writings on economic and social
policy, which blamed the expansion of the social services for all the
nation's economic ills. The Heath government attracted particular

criticism for its use of employment in the social services as a cheap way of following a full-employment policy. Bacon and Eltis castigated government for increasing the number of 'civil servants, social workers, and most teachers and medical workers' whose salaries are drawn from the 'marketed output of industry and services'.[8] They blamed this, more than any other factor, for what they saw as Britain's major economic problem — 'too few producers'.

I hope that I have already shown that this argument blames the egg for the chicken. Employment in productive industry was declining for at least five years before the major expansion of the social services; the Heath government's response was a reluctant and somewhat desperate one in the face of mounting unemployment. But even better evidence of the fallacies in Bacon and Eltis's arguments are provided by an analysis of the consequences of changes in policy that have occurred since 1975.

The Labour government tried hard to release resources from the social services, and to stimulate the growth of productive industry. It succeeded in cutting expenditure, particularly on capital projects, and it also achieved some reductions in the social services workforce. But the results of these policies, and its other cuts in public spending, were higher rates of unemployment. Resources were not redeployed in productive industry in the way in which Bacon and Eltis's model would require. Where increased investment occurred, it did not add to the productive workforce. New plant was used to increase productivity and reduce labour costs. Consequently, even when government was trying to reduce its role as a provider of social services, it was drawn into increased provision for the unemployed and low-income families.

These results of attempts to cut spending on social services demonstrate the futility of such efforts at a time when the main function of social services is to provide an income to the growing proportion of non-productive members of the community. It is a necessary consequence of the 'Ricardo phenomenon' that productive industry distributes less and less of its output to workers, and that output does not grow. Under these circumstances, government is forced in one way or another to do something to provide subsistence incomes to people who are put out of work, or who do not earn enough from work. The Heath government attempted to achieve this by Keynesian methods; the Labour government abandoned these and adopted a modified monetarist approach. But both were forced to provide direct subsidies to a sizeable proportion of the population, by means of transfer payments; and both were forced to maintain a large workforce in the social services, as an alternative to even higher unemployment.

Apart from demographic changes and the relative price effect, the main cause of the growth of social services expenditure was the failure of the productive system to distribute incomes for consumption. However it goes about the task, government's main role under these circumstances is to raise sufficient money from those who are in productive employment to provide incomes for those who are not. But the vast majority of taxation throughout this period was on incomes and on consumption, and not on profits or production. The figures given in Table 7.3 show that income tax grew in the 1970s, while corporation tax declined; and employees continued to contribute more than twice as much to the National Insurance Fund as employers.[9]

Table 7.3

Government receipts (£m., at 1975 prices) from	1971	1975	1978
Income taxes	10,822	14,422	13,129
Index of income taxes	75.0	100.0	91.0
Corporation tax	2,562	2,235	2,462
Index of corporation tax	114.6	100.0	110.2
National Insurance contributions (from employers)	2,188	3,741	3,820
National Insurance contributions (from employees)	5,178	7,619	8,039

Two myths about British taxation should be exploded at this point. First, Britain does not impose an above average burden on its citizens when compared with other industrialised countries. As a proportion of GDP, British taxes are considerably lower than those of several EEC countries, particularly the Scandanavian countries and the Netherlands.[10] Second, the combined effect of all the various forms of taxation is only moderately progressive. National Insurance contributions and taxes on consumption fall disproportionately on the poorest sectors of the population, and cancel out a good deal of the progressive effect of income taxes. Hence the vast bulk of transfer payments in Britain consist of taxes on the spending power of ordinary wage- and salary-earners, which are then redistributed to non-employed citizens and very low-wage earners.

As the 'Ricardo phenomenon' has developed, this process has become a more important feature of the role of government. In 1966, transfers were only 8.9 per cent of GDP; by 1978, they were 13.3 per cent. But the expansion of transfers would have been even more marked if governments had attempted to adhere to the principles of the Beveridge Welfare State. In fact, although both parties in opposition have argued for improved universal social security benefits, in power they have increasingly used selective, means-tested systems of transfer payments. In line with changes in this direction, resentment against the beneficiaries of state transfers has increased. This has been particularly the case as, with increasing unemployment and below subsistence earnings, the state has been forced to increase its income maintenance role in relation to people of working age.

(iii) Family poverty and the Conservative government

In the 1970 election campaign, family poverty was an issue, and the Conservatives made some capital out of Labour's discomfort over it by pledging to improve family allowances. During the election, Edward Heath wrote to the CPAG 'We accept that . . . the only way of tackling family poverty in the short term is to increase family allowances and operate the clawback principle.'[11]

In fact, within five months of taking office, the Conservatives introduced Family Income Supplements, based on a quite different principle – the subsidisation of poverty-level wages. (As the previous Labour government had found over the income guarantee, it is virtually impossible for a new administration to frame legislation so quickly – and the Conservatives had not apparently even planned it. This gives rise to the suspicion – confirmed by one ex-minister – that Labour had drafted legislation for Family Income Supplements before they left office.)

Family Income Supplements were, in effect, means-tested benefits for people in full-time employment with one or more children. The government laid down a scale of 'prescribed earnings' (which varied with the number of children) below which the family qualified for a supplement to their wages. The amount of assistance given was extremely small – the original scheme cost only £8 million – but for a government which had promised to control public spending this had the advantage of being the cheapest way of 'doing something about family poverty'.

The scheme had all the disadvantages of a means-tested system: stigma, complexity, and a bureaucratic assessment procedure. It also created a 'poverty trap', as low-wage earners lost benefit when their earnings increased. The government could have given far more effective and acceptable help to low-income families by raising the tax threshold, so that the poorest tax payers were exempted, and increasing family allowances with clawback. At the same time as Family Income Supplements were introduced, income tax was cut by 2½p, giving back over £300 million to taxpayers, but very little of this to poor families.

Family Income Supplements marked the beginning of a new phase in social policy, whose philosophy Sir Keith Joseph, as Secretary of State for Health and Social Security, justified in his theory of the 'cycle of deprivation'. According to this, the aim of official interventions should be to break a vicious circle that occurred when 'there is a combination of bad factors — problems associated with poverty, poor housing and large family size, for example.'[12] The cycle of deprivation was supposed to explain the persistence of poverty in the midst of affluence, to show 'why . . . in spite of long periods of full employment and relative prosperity and the improvement in community services . . . deprivation and problems of maladjustment so conspicuously persist.'[13] Sir Keith argued that poor families reared children who were in turn both poor and maladjusted; that the culture of poverty caused intergenerational continuities of both deviance and deprivation:[14]

> Deprivation takes many forms, and they interact. It shows itself for example in poverty, in emotional impoverishment, in personality disorder, in poor educational attainment, in depression and despair. . . . It is where there is a combination of bad factors . . . that children are most at risk.

Hence what was needed was not simply material aid; it was also official surveillance and, in many cases, detailed supervision of parental performance.

Introducing the Family Income Supplements Bill, Sir Keith commented that[15]

> We hope to use it to provide a passport for the poorest to all the remission available. It will give us contact with the poorest working

class households, about whom far too little is known, and give us knowledge to ensure these families apply for . . . other benefits.

He promised another complementary means-tested scheme for rent rebates, which was brought in the following year. The effect of these measures was to create an identifiable class of poor families, whose distinguishing feature was that they had to claim special assistance to achieve a subsistence income, even when they were in work; and who were forced into continual contact with a swelling social services bureaucracy, which assessed them for each of a number of needs. Both the new schemes were very labour intensive, by the standards of income maintenance provision. The Family Income Supplements cost over £600,000 to distribute £8 million in benefits. Later schemes, such as those that gave small amounts of cheaper meat and butter to those entitled to other means-tested assistance, were even more costly to administer.

Within this class of poor families there was another, singled out by policy for even closer supervision. With the creation of the local authority social services departments in 1971, there existed a new agency which combined some general responsibilities for welfare in the community with a number of detailed powers to intervene in families (compulsorily, if necessary), to monitor or control behaviour and to remove deviants or rescue victims. Ever since the mid-1960s, social workers had been increasingly involved in work with families aimed at preventing their breakup through conflict, debt or eviction, and specifically at forestalling the reception of children into care. Section One of the Children and Young Persons Act (1963), enabled local authorities to make such interventions, and gave them very limited powers to provide financial assistance. By 1972, 247,556 families received advice, assistance or small payments from social workers under this Section in England alone.[16] Most of these were referred by the major social services – health, education, housing or social security – as people requiring some kind of extra surveillance, guidance or control, or as needing more assistance than they were willing to provide.

In fact, this led to the creation of a new category of 'welfare cases' – effectively an even more stigmatised group than those on means-tested benefits. In exchange for very limited material assistance, 'welfare cases' were expected to have their family relationship scrutinised by social workers, who had powers to compel changes in behaviour.

This development conformed perfectly to the 'cycle of deprivation' model, which insisted that only in this very detailed and personal way could the patterns that led to persistent poverty and deviance be broken. The prevalence of this model of social control will be discussed more fully in the next chapter.

The 'cycle of deprivation' theory was really a pessimistic version of the philosophy that inspired 'positive discrimination'. It was similar in its emphasis on the combination and interaction of negative factors, and the need to do something more about these than universalist principles allowed. However, it attached no importance to the problems of stigma, frustration and resentment among those who received such small amounts of assistance on such paternalistic terms; nor did it take account of the dangers of a backlash from tax-paying and rate-paying workers, who saw these measures as selecting the least deserving for special attention. The Conservatives were later to exploit the least popular features of the systems they introduced into their campaigns against waste in the Welfare State, and their arguments about its demoralising effects on the poor. By the time Sir Keith Joseph had announced, in 1978, that the cycle of deprivation was a myth, and had never existed, the services it inspired had become integral features of the Welfare State.

(iv) The social wage

The main features of Conservative social policy were the rapid expansion of low-wage employment in the social services, and the proliferation of means-tested benefits. In some cases these two developments were ludicrously combined: many of the new staff taken on to administer selective income maintenance provisions had themselves to claim Family Income Supplements.

As part of its Social Contract with the trade unions, Labour pledged itself in the first 1974 election to do something about long-overdue reforms of universal social security benefits. As was the case ten years previously, the party's main emphasis was on the needs of the elderly. The Conservatives had introduced an optional 'state reserve' scheme, which was to provide earnings-related pensions for those not covered by occupational schemes, but it was never implemented. Labour scrapped this, and brought in a more comprehensive measure, based on a new system of weekly wage-related contributions — thus finally achieving what it had been promising since 1957. The new government also raised the value of pensions immediately, and pegged annual increases to the rise in wages or prices, whichever was the greater. Third, Labour introduced a new scheme for child benefits (including the first child in the family) which replaced family allowances and tax allowances for children. This was an overdue rationalisation of the system, but did not significantly alter Britain's relative position, at the bottom of the European league table in provision for income maintenance for children.

The Social Contract represented a temporary refocusing of attention on universal benefits, and the underlying principles of social security provision. However, it was far from radical; it saw no need to improve the coverage for people of working age, or to question Beveridge's notion that social security was intended to cover 'interruptions in or cessation of earnings'. Labour talked vaguely about redistributing income and wealth in the 1974 elections, but put forward no clear plans for doing so.

With the Social Contract came the notion of the social wage. This concept had some potential importance, in that it recognised the role of government in maintaining the standards of living of all its citizens — which in turn could have been used to grasp the notion that this was increasingly important in the age of automation, when wages and salaries were providing a diminishing proportion of the income necessary for that standard of living. However, in the hands of Labour ministers, the social wage was a tool with much more pragmatic uses. Denis Healey employed the concept mainly in order to argue for the 'voluntary' incomes policy imposed in the summer of 1975.

If the Labour government had fully accepted the implications of the notion of a social wage, it might have argued consistently for restraint on pay claims. It could have pointed out that there were opportunities for the steady increase in the value of income maintenance and social services provision for its citizens by the state, arising from higher productivity. But it would then have had to show how *all* could benefit from these changes. Instead, Denis Healey stated vaguely in his 1975 Budget speech that the social wage was then worth the equivalent of £1,000 for every adult member of the working population in the UK.[17] To make this sound like a convincing case for pay restraint, he would have needed to define how automation would lead to improved productivity which would create less work; and how it was therefore more appropriate for the social wage to increase than the money wages of workers. Listening to Denis Healey's speech, people in employment had every reason to be suspicious of his motives. He was in fact giving notice of the government's intention to restrain pay increases without a compensatory increase in the social wage for all; indeed, of a determined effort to reduce the value of the social wage.

For, in spite of its high-sounding phrases in the 1974 elections, the Labour leadership had by no means been converted to the idea that the government should play an increased role in maintaining the incomes of the working population. Rather, it was rapidly shifting its priorities back to where they had been throughout its previous period of office — towards industrial expansion. In its White Paper 'The Government's Expenditure Plans' (published in 1976), it stated baldly: 'Within total public expenditure, a higher priority is being given to expenditure which is designed to maintain or improve our industrial capability.'[18] Far from attempting to justify an increased role in providing incomes for people of working age, it justified its plans for cutting social services spending in terms of restoring 'an appropriate balance' (i.e. less state provision) between earnings from employment and the social wage. The White Paper of 1977 continued:[19]

> The objectives of that plan were to make possible a shift of resources
> into industrial investment and exports; to restrain the increase in
> the burden of taxation which would otherwise have been necessary;
> to maintain an appropriate balance between take-home pay and the
> provision of public services; and by these means to reduce inflation-
> ary pressure in the economy.

Thus the Labour leadership paved the way for the new Conservative approach, emphasising the necessity for more investment in private industry, and for reductions in social services provision to release resources for achieving this. At the same time, Labour failed to restructure the income maintenance system in line with the important changes that had been taking place in the 1970s. This in turn provided the Conservatives with opportunities to dismantle parts of the social security system, which had fallen into decay.

(v) Neglect of the social security system

Ever since 1968, there had been a rapid growth in the numbers of unemployed and single-parent claimants of supplementary benefits. By 1975, reforms in the whole system of social security provision for the long-term unemployed and for single parents were urgently required. But Labour procrastinated and evaded these issues, and eventually did nothing except review the supplementary benefits scheme – which provided the Conservatives with a blueprint for their programme of cuts in social security benefits.

In 1974, the Finer Committee reported on the situation of one-parent families in Britain. Among its many recommendations for change was one concerning income maintenance. After criticising the insecure and inconsistent basis of provision for such families under supplementary benefits, it made recommendations for very modest changes in the direction of providing a guaranteed maintenance allowance, to secure a minimum weekly income for single parents. The Finer scheme retained the means-test and cohabitation rule, and was still to be administered by the Supplementary Benefits Commission; yet even these minor changes were not acceptable to the government, and the report's recommendations on income maintenance were not implemented.

In 1977, the Supplementary Benefits Commission's Chairman, David Donnison, began to campaign for long-term rates of supplementary benefit for people who were unemployed for more than two years. Under existing regulations, the unemployed could never qualify for these higher rates of weekly benefit, which were considered essential for other groups of long-term claimants. The Supplementary Benefits Commission's own researches had revealed that the unemployed were the group of claimants with the fewest resources in savings and material possessions; consequently, they were actually in greater need of the higher rates than other groups. Yet Donnison's pleas for this minor alteration in the regulations fell on deaf ears: nothing was done about the long-term unemployed.

By 1978, the position had worsened further. The expansion in the number of claimants in these two categories can be seen from the figures given in Table 7.4.[20] There was clearly a strong case for a new structure of universal benefits, providing longer-term cover for unemployment, and a minimum income for single parents. The real reason why the Labour government was unwilling to take action

Table 7.4

	1973	1974	1975	1976	1977
Unemployed claimants of supplementary benefits (thousands)	249	301	541	654	703
Single-parent claimants of supplementary benefits (thousands)	228	245	276	303	323

was its commitment to the traditional aims of social policy — to reducing the role of the state in income maintenance, and concentrating on industrial expansion. Having declared its priorities in this direction, it could not provide long-term support for people of working age as a substitute for earnings from work.

Undoubtedly, it would also have been politically disastrous to do so. Throughout the 1970s, there was a mounting crescendo of protest from people in employment about the 'abuse' of the social security system. Orchestrated by right-wing politicians and the popular Press, the 'anti-scroungers' campaign gained momentum during this period, and the unemployed and single parents were particular objects for obloquy. The Supplementary Benefits Commission responded with a greater emphasis on the detection of fraud, through the appointment of more and more special investigators, but this only seemed to confirm suspicion and resentment about claimants, particularly the able-bodied of working age.

It is significant that research done in the EEC, and published in 1977, discovered that the British public was far more resentful of income maintenance assistance to the poor than any other European nation, and blamed the poor more for their plight than any other. Yet in many ways this vindictiveness was simply a reflection of government priorities and policies in the late 1970s. The Labour government made it clear that its priority was to reduce provision for state maintenance, and to increase the share of income coming from work. This would have been fair enough if they had been able to promote a more rapid rate of growth, and expand employment. But such a policy without significant growth, and with unemployment of nearly 1.5 million, gave the strong impression that those requiring income maintenance support were a burden upon those in work, and were causing Britain's economic problems. The Conservatives merely took this philosophy a stage further.

Because of the neglect of social security provision for the unemployed and single parents, an impossible strain was placed on supplementary benefits. As described in the last chapter, they represented an unsatisfactory compromise, hastily assembled in the mid-1960s, to try to give National Assistance a certain respectability. They had been adapted to the needs of long-term claimants with unchanging circumstances, and particularly to the elderly. Administrative changes had reduced their flexibility and responsiveness to the needs of young families, and particularly those of the poorest claimants, who were subject to recurring financial crises; yet these were precisely the groups whose numbers had been increasing, whereas the numbers of claimants who were pensioners, disabled or sick had slightly declined. The Labour government set up a team of civil servants, in 1977, to review the workings of the supplementary benefits scheme, and to report on how it might be improved without extra cost to the taxpayer.

The task was, in fact, quite impossible. The failures of the supplementary benefits scheme stemmed directly from the failures of National Insurance benefits to provide adequate universal cover against the exigencies of modern economic forces. Supplementary benefits were being required to do at least three different things which, if not incompatible, were certainly difficult to reconcile within the same organisational structure. They were being required to provide regular weekly supplements to nearly 2 million elderly claimants, without excessive stigma or frequent detailed surveillance. They were also required to assess and respond to occasional requests for short-term assistance by about 1 million claimants of working age every year — a task requiring a high ratio of staff-time and individual attention. Finally, they were required to provide medium-term assistance to many couples and families living in extreme poverty, who, in addition to regular weekly payments, needed occasional additional help to ward off debt, eviction or fuel disconnection. Because the scheme had been reorganised since 1966 mainly for the first task, it was under-staffed and ill-equipped for the second and third, and these tasks were unpopular, and badly done. Only two solutions could have resolved the problem: either higher rates of benefit had to remove the neediness of those claimants who demanded individual attention; or staffing had to be increased to do the job of meeting individual need more efficiently. The no-cost basis of the review ruled out both alternatives.

Accordingly, when the review was published, in 1978, it produced a non-solution. Supplementary benefits were to be adapted to their 'mass role' (the support of about 3 million claimants and another 2 million dependants) by removing a great deal of their discretion to provide extra help in cases of hardship. By making regulations which fixed sums to be paid in certain limited 'prescribed circumstances', the whole system could be made 'simpler and clearer'.[21] The unpopular and staff-intensive task of assessing the individual needs of the poorest claimants could be abolished by administrative fiat; this would entail an element of 'rough justice', but it would lead to a more comprehensible system for all.

These changes were very much in line with the spirit of income maintenance policy of the previous three years. The Labour government had turned its back on the notion of expanding the social wage with increases in productivity. It had excluded the possibility of extending the coverage of universal benefits. It was determined to save money wherever possible in the income maintenance field. These 'reforms' of supplementary benefits were in fact cuts, aimed at saving hundreds of staff and millions of pounds in benefits. The fact that they were to be made at the expense of the very poorest group of claimants was unfortunate. Their purpose was twofold: to save expense and to consolidate the position of supplementary benefits as the ground-floor of the income maintenance edifice. Instead of a residual safety net, as Beveridge had intended, the means-tested scheme, derived from the Poor Law, was to be the base on which the whole social security system rested.

8 Social control

(i) The political definition of social problems

So far I have argued that social policies in the period I have analysed were determined largely by economic forces. I have suggested that they represented, to a great extent, unplanned government reactions to the social consequences of the 'Ricardo phenomenon'. However, economic factors alone do not determine social policies. The politics of social policy shape the choices that are available; the political process provides the opportunities for change, and the arena for conflict.

In this chapter, I shall consider the political definition of 'social problems', and how it affects the way in which social services are provided. I shall argue that between the mid-1960s and the present day, certain key decisions were made about how poverty, unemployment, family breakup, child deprivation and adolescent unruliness were to be perceived and treated. The definitions of all these 'problems' were subtly or dramatically altered, with far-reaching consequences for the services used to deal with them. For much of the period, a degree of consensus between the two major parties obscured the importance of the changes that were taking place.

As part of that consensus in the late 1960s and early 1970s, poverty came to be seen as a condition of certain individuals and families – to be tackled by selective benefits, rebates and supplements – and not as a structural feature of the economy, to be tackled by minimum wages, universal dividends or increased family allowances. Unemployment came to be accepted as part of the temporary price paid for higher productivity, a problem which would soon evaporate when the modernisation of industry was completed. Unemployment was to be softened by redundancy payments and earnings-related benefits, but there was

143

to be no provision for its long-term effects. Family breakup was condoned by the state, but provision for unsupported mothers was strictly limited and conditional; it put more emphasis on policing benefits than on compensating for disadvantages. Deprived children were seen as best helped by monitoring parental performance, and giving a certain amount of material assistance to parents defined as inadequate or immature. Delinquency was seen as a manifestation of much the same family structure and material conditions as deprivation, and provision for delinquents was merged with provision for deprived children.

All these definitions were new, and all involved expansions of state provision, but the greatest growth was in services that required considerable individual inquiry, intervention and supervision. For instance, between 1967 and 1977, the numbers of claimants of supplementary benefits increased from approximately 2.5 million to 3 million. But the numbers of *staff* employed in supplementary benefits in the same period increased from 12,000 to 30,000. Although supplementary benefits pay out only 14.5 per cent of the social security budget, they now account for half the total of local office staff. Similarly, the numbers of social workers doubled between 1968 and 1974.

This form of expansion of the social services defined certain individuals and families as targets for particular kinds of labour-intensive state interventions. The targets were mainly people who were becoming marginal to the economy as producers, but who still had a certain importance as consumers. New definitions of poverty and deprivation ensured that their incomes did not fall below certain levels, but effectively excluded them, for the time being or permanently, from any share in the growing affluence of other sectors of the economy. The method of intervention chosen created opportunities for white-collar employment in the public sector, at a time when productive industry was reducing its workforce. It also allowed the creation of a number of large-scale organisations in the social services, which in turn gave further chances of careers in middle and upper management.

Initially, the role of this new corps of social welfare officials was presented in optimistic and creative terms. They were engaged in exercises of 'positive discrimination'; the social workers among them were 'preventing' family breakup, deprivation and delinquency; the community workers were ensuring 'participation'. In the early 1970s, these labels started to disappear. Since the mid-1970s, their roles have been fairly suddenly redefined in terms of rationing scarce resources, detecting 'abuse', and controlling deviant behaviour. The process of redefinition has been political. The same target groups which were originally seen as especially in need of many kinds of assistance were all at once seen as particularly morally suspect. It was precisely the fact that they required state aid that was seen as undermining their desire to work and to take responsibility for their families.

Yet there has been no fundamental discontinuity in policy; rather an accelerating slide from one official perception of the problems to the next. The fact is that all were ways of controlling people who had been excluded from a share of economic progress. The Labour governments of the 1960s offered 'extra help to the neediest'. The Heath Conservatives (Sir Keith Joseph, mark one) claimed that these same people were also the most deviant — and likely to bring up their children to be the same unless they got extra supervision as well as assistance. Their Labour successors placed more emphasis on the control of deviance, and the need for strict rationing of resources. The new Conservative approach is to cut state provision, remoralise the poor, and promote law and order (Sir Keith Joseph, mark two).

These political definitions affect both public opinion and the behaviour of officials in the social services, through a process which has been referred to as 'ideological domination'. As government policies change, the attitudes towards target groups that underlie them are spread through official publications and through the media. This pervasive spread of new attitudes (or, in many cases, old prejudices which can be traced to the Poor Law and beyond) in turn legitimate official policies. Workers in the social services are caught up in the same process of influence, and their dealings with claimants and clients are shaped by the same forces. I shall argue that, far from constituting an effective professional or trade union resistance against ideological domination, social services workers more often reflect official definitions of problems, and uncritically act as agents of new policies, however restrictive or controlling they may be. The field of child care and delinquency provides a case study in such ideological domination, which will be considered later in this chapter.

(ii) Paternalism

The dominant model of social provision and social control in the early 1970s was paternalism. It is worth considering the ideological basis of paternalism in some detail, as it manifested itself in all the social services at that time, and its shortcomings largely exposed those services to attacks by the radical Right, which espoused the historical antithesis of paternalism — economic liberalism. What follows is a simplified model of paternalism — an 'ideal type' of this ideology of social polciy — not perfectly reflected in any one government minister or any particular agency at any moment of time.

In essence, paternalism starts from the proposition that state assistance is for the casualties of economic growth and progress — either for those who cannot compete at all, or for those who cannot keep up in a competitive race. In the immediate post-war era, the Beveridge principle had been used to identify *situations* in which citizens could not support themselves ('interruptions in or cessation of earnings'), and then give an equal amount of assistance to *all* citizens in such situations. Paternalism tries to identify *individuals* who cannot cope, whatever their situation, and to give them help based on *needs*. It implies that the state has a duty to assist, but that the duty stems from the neediness, and hence, implicitly, the inadequacy of the recipient. Thus assistance is not confined to the elderly, the sick and the unemployed; limited aid is also given to people in work, in the form of rebates and income supplements — but only if their wages are calculated to fall short of their requirements according to certain scales. In practice, therefore, paternalism is always applying a means test (or several means tests) to worse-off citizens, measuring their eligibility for assistance. It invites them to be constantly assessed and reassessed for their neediness, both when they are in work and when they are not earning. It prescribes amounts that determine the ceilings of their incomes. Paternalism's trap is that, having once qualified for its assistance, it requires either sacrifice or considerable effort to re-achieve independence, because a small increase in income from earnings results in a similar loss of benefits.

Paternalism implies that social control should be exercised as part and parcel of the process of material assistance. Since the poor and the deviant are seen as heavily overlapping groups (cf. the 'cycle of deprivation', see Chapter 7), assistance should not be given without supervision, and vice versa. Paternalism tends to assume that control can either be exercised without it being noticed (because it is helpful and benevolent); or that if it is noticed, the client will be able to see that it is for his own good. Hence paternalism seldom recognises conflicts of interest between the individual and the state. For instance, in cases of neglected or abused children, it suggests that there is no real clash of interest between parent and child, or the state and parent, and that such situations can be resolved by judicious handouts from the welfare parlour. The controls that paternalism prefers are covert and manipulative. The purposes and consequences of its methods (rationing, supervision) are seldom acknowledged to the client. It assumes that alterations of environmental circumstances and other manipulations of external factors can alter feelings, attitudes, behaviour and relationships. It suggests that the use of limited assistance and monitoring can remove the need to make judgments or decisions, and to confront issues of principle. In short, it believes that social problems – whether of poverty or deviant behaviour (and usually, as it sees them, of people who are both poor and deviant) – can be *managed* and *treated* in such a way that they are brought under control. Paternalism denies the effectiveness of clear-cut rules or punishments for their infraction. However, it relies heavily (though covertly) on punishment to back up its 'benevolent' controls; and the use of punishment tends to grow insidiously within every aspect of the paternalistic system. The juvenile justice system in this country is a case in point (see pp. 155-6, below).

Paternalism applies equally to the provision of selective benefits, and to attempts to prevent such problems as family breakup, child deprivation and delinquency. Indeed, it tries ideally to combine elements of assistance and individual supervision in all its interventions. Consequently, it particularly favours the use of social work as a means of dealing with social problems; and it especially approves of the selection of a large category of 'welfare cases', whose extra neediness betrays their faulty psychic adjustment. If the major social services cater for categories of people who can get by with standard selective provision, the personal social services exist to modify the behaviour and the needs of a large group who find life difficult in spite of receiving this standard ration. Hence paternalism was willing to sponsor the very rapid growth of local authority social services departments in the early 1970s, and to encourage the major social services to identify 'welfare cases', and refer more and more of them to social workers for their special brand of behavioural manipulation. Social work's own ideology runs counter to paternalism in many ways, but it allowed itself to be moulded by the dominant political ethos of the era in which it was being expanded. Indeed, social work became the fulcrum of the paternalistic system, in that its role was to control the behaviour of people who did not react as expected to the benevolence of the other social agencies.

(iii) The destruction of the paternalist myth

Although the above summary is necessarily a caricature, it none the less highlights the essential features of the paternalist ideology. Baldly stated, paternalism rests on the myth that vast human problems — like poverty, idleness, family disruption, parental violence and adolescent unrest — can be contained, or even reduced, by large numbers of low-grade officials dispensing limited benefits and services. If anybody working in the social services ever believed this myth when they took their jobs, they soon had their faith challenged by experience; yet this was essentially the ideological base on which the selective income maintenance system and the personal social services were expanded. It is little wonder that government and officialdom soon stopped talking about *conquering* poverty, or *preventing* family breakups, or *reducing* juvenile delinquency (as they had done in the 1960s). Yet the original myth was never repudiated, and both government and officialdom bought into this false basis for building an empire which could never be defended.

The fallacy behind that whole empire was that if the state gave needy and difficult people some limited benefits and services they would become more tractable. More social services would mean a better-behaved populace; more expenditure would mean more effective social control. Yet the truth is that there is no necessary or direct connection between social welfare provision and contentment or pliable behaviour. Industrial malaise, unemployment, disillusion with family life, frustration among young people, are far more potent social forces than any that can be mustered from an office block in the city centre. Indeed, the manner in which many of these services were given (involving complexity, suspicion, bureaucratic delay, mystification, evasion or insincere 'caring') often contributed to the frustration that led to more deviant behaviour, or more insistent demands.

Paternalism was always vulnerable to an attack by its historical antithesis, the ideology of the 1834 Poor Law. Sir Keith Joseph, who was one of paternalism's most persuasive spokesmen, became (in a Damascus-like conversion) one of its most destructive critics. In his notorious speech on the birth-rate, in October 1974, he denounced the paternalist myth of control through state assistance:[1]

> We were taught that crime, violence, wife-beating, child-beating, were the result of poverty; abolish poverty and they would disappear. By now we are in a position to test all these fine theories. . . . Real incomes per head have risen beyond what anyone dreamed of a generation back; so have education budgets and welfare budgets; so also have delinquency, truancy, vandalism, hooliganism, illiteracy, decline in educational standards. . . . The only real lasting help we can give to the poor is helping them to help themselves; to do the opposite, to create more dependence, is to destroy them morally, while throwing an unfair burden on society. . . . When you take responsibility away from people, you make them irresponsible. Hand in hand with this, you break down traditional morals.

Once the Conservatives had acknowledged that their own expansion of the social services under Heath's government had not produced more effective social control, they freed themselves to make drastic cuts in state provision. If more services did not make people more contented and well behaved, there was no reason to suppose that fewer services would make them less so. Indeed, Sir Keith Joseph's speeches harked back to the 1834 tradition when he suggested that cuts in benefits would actually improve people's morals. The social and economic implications of the Conservative cuts in social services expenditure will be discussed in the next chapter. My purpose in this section is to examine the ideological basis of the new Conservative approach to social control, and to consider its effects on the personal social services.

An important part of the Conservatives' renunciation of paternalism was their rejection of social engineering and manipulation. They reinstated the notions of deservingness and punishment, and revived the moral basis of social policy. The new Conservative ideology insists that state provision should only be for people who really cannot help themselves. This alone should be the group which deserves state assistance. The question of who is and who is not deserving is a moral and political one, but it is susceptible to clear-cut definition and decision. By making controls far more overt, they can be made more acceptable. Moral rules are self-evident truths; even the poor can perceive their basis, and respect them, even when they lose their livelihood in the process. Indeed they can benefit from such an experience — it remoralises them for the struggle for survival which is the only true test of a man's worth.

The new Conservative ideology prescribes traditional moral imperatives — the work ethic, family responsibility, law and order — which apply to all, irrespective of their situations. It recognises no exceptions, and allows no mitigation from circumstances. It implies that help should only be given to those who can prove their moral credentials. Unlike paternalism, it suggests that control should be visible and conscious, and quite distinct from assistance.

The new ideology reinstates punishment as an overt means of control. It suggests that specific penalties should be attached to particular offences against its rules, and that offenders should be disciplined into better behaviour by largely impersonal processes. It argues that harsh treatment for a few deviants is for the greater good of the many who will be deterred into conformity with official standards. It has little use for social work, which is seen as potentially corrupting in its insistence on individualised justice and the relevance of social factors in problem behaviour.

Despite the apparent polarisation of the two ideologies, there has been no sudden break between the application of paternalism to our social services, and the return to the principles of 1834. Under the Labour governments of 1974 and 1979, a heavy emphasis on the scarcity of resources introduced strong moral overtones into questions of social priority, and notions of relative deservingness returned in all but name. Similarly, the failure of paternalistic measures of social control led to an increasing emphasis on 'structured containment', for instance in juvenile delinquency, which was simply punishment in poor disguise. A good example of the drift from paternalism towards the new Conservative philosophy was the 'Review of the Supplementary Benefits Scheme' in 1978. In its insistence on published regulations, on simplicity, on the unsoundness of arguments from hardship, on fairness as between claimants rather than individualised assessment, and on the capacity of those suffering official deprivation to see the 'rough justice' in their hunger, the document anticipated the ideology of the Conservative government — which in turn eagerly embraced its recommendations.

(iv) Family breakup

One example of the application of these ideologies to the definition of social problems is to be found in policy over family breakup. In the 1960s, middle-class attitudes towards the role of women and the individual's right to self-fulfilment moved (superficially at least) in the direction of equality and freedom, and this was reflected in laws which permitted easier divorce, and allowed for more equal property rights. But as the Finer Report showed, the 'lower orders' by no means received the full benefits of these changes. Marital breakdown in working-class families continued to be dealt with mainly in the magistrates' courts, under different and more traditional legislation, and issues of income and property by the local authority housing departments and the Supplementary Benefits Commission – agencies which embodied paternalistic principles.

This is still clearly reflected in the conditions under which supplementary benefits are provided for unsupported mothers. In principle, the state considers that the income for rearing children should be provided by their father, from wages earned in employment. The state is willing to supplement these earnings in certain circumstances, or provide temporary relief during unemployment. But it does not recognise a role for itself in making a major contribution to the cost of child-rearing – as in France, for instance, where family allowances are many times higher than in Britain. In practice, however, some couples separate in circumstances that do not allow the father to give adequate financial support to his children, and in these situations the state (apart from pursuing the father to maximise his contributions) is also willing to give limited and conditional assistance to the mother (who in the vast majority of cases retains responsibility for their care).

The conditions attached to assistance reveal paternalism's attitude towards the mother's social role. The state, in effect, takes over the role of a mean and jealous husband. It will provide a subsistence income, but in return it expects fidelity. To qualify for this income, the woman must not 'cohabit' with another man. In practice, this means that the Supplementary Benefits Commission will investigate any complaint that men have been seen regularly entering her house; also, her subsistence will be removed if there is suspicion that she *could* demand financial support in return for any association with a man, whether she is actually getting such support or not. Far from promoting the freedom of a divorced or separated woman to live as she chooses, or giving her an income as a right during her children's dependence on her, the state is willing to take responsibility only if she adopts the most traditional form of dependent relationship with itself, a suspicious and penny-pinching husband. Furthermore, if she works to try to be independent it traps her in her poverty. In 1978, if a single parent with two small children, earning £35 a week and getting all her entitlements to selective benefits, received a £20 pay rise, she would end up only £1.05 better off as a result.

In the 1960s and early 1970s, provision for single parents through the supplementary benefits scheme increased in line with the higher rate of divorce and separation. But paternalist principles never conceded a true right to benefit for mothers bringing up children alone. The rules of supplementary benefits still reinforced the notion that fathers should work to support their children, and mothers should depend on their husbands, and claim from them. As numbers on supplementary benefit grew, so did official suspicion and fear of 'abuse'; the cohabitation rule was more watchfully enforced. The Finer Report recommended the retention of this rule, on the grounds that its abolition would make separated mothers better off than married ones; yet its very modest recommendations for improvements in single parents' rights to assistance have not been implemented. Instead, the restrictive rules and rationing procedures recommended by the Supplementary Benefits review have been incorporated into the 1980 Social Security Act, and paternalistic provision has merged into the harshness of the new Conservative principles.

At the same time as numbers of single parents on supplementary benefits were increasing, so were interventions into families by social workers. The 1963 Children and Young Persons Act prescribed the wider use of social work to assist families in which there were children 'at risk' of coming into care. In the last chapter, I mentioned the rapid expansion of such interventions, and the mushroom growth of limited financial aid under Section One of that Act, between the mid-1960s and the mid-1970s. Social workers combined powers to make detailed individual assessments of material needs with powers to supervise parental performance — a characteristic blend in paternalist policy. It is clear from the statistics on divorce and separation that they did not succeed in 'preventing' family breakup in this sense. However, for several years interventions in families increased rapidly without any rise in the numbers of children coming into care. But in 1973 there occurred a scandal that radically altered the whole role of local authority social work – the Maria Colwell case. From this point onwards, the paternalistic role of 'supporting' children in difficult families rapidly gave way to a more coercive role of 'rescuing' them from potentially damaging parents. Instead of being involved in preventing family breakup, social workers were increasingly required to control deviant parents and remove vulnerable children – a task far more in keeping with the requirements of the new Conservatism. The expression 'child at risk' ceased to mean 'child at risk of coming into care'; instead, it meant 'child at risk of being harmed by his parents'.

(v) Child abuse

Social workers had always recognised some families which were damaging or destructive to their children, and that it was part of their task to identify such families, and take decisive action to protect these children. However, the ideology of paternalism worked against clarity, firmness or honesty in such cases, suggesting that even the worst families might improve with limited material assistance and close supervision. Hence, in a large number of cases parents suspected of cruelty or neglect were never told that this was the reason why social workers visited them: the whole issue of the child's welfare was fudged, in a vague welter of 'assistance and support'.

Thus when Maria Colwell died at the hands of her stepfather, after having been returned to her mother under social work supervision, this was not an isolated case of poor judgment, woolly thinking and shoddy practice in issues of this sort. However, it would have been unlikely to have attracted much attention, but for the intervention of the Secretary of State for Health and Social Security. When Maria died, her death received no national publicity; when her stepfather was sentenced, the Press gave the case very little coverage. But when Sir Keith Joseph set up an inquiry into her death, and made an important speech linking it with social policy, the Maria Colwell case became a public scandal.[2] This was a clear example of the political definition of social problems; child abuse became *the* issue of local authority social work from the moment that Sir Keith Joseph drew attention to it.

The expansion – and elasticity – of official estimates of child abuse are illustrated by the numbers and variations in the 'At Risk' registers set up by local authorities after the Maria Colwell inquiry. There is no strong reason for supposing that parents were more cruel to children after 1974 than they had been before, and still less for believing that there are high concentrations of cruel parents in East Sussex, and hardly any in Somerset. Yet East Sussex had 1,500 children on its register out of a total population of 660,000, while Somerset, with a population of about 410,000, had only 30 children on its register.[3] Stevenson and Hallett found no demographic explanation for the fact that some areas had fewer than 10 and others more than 100 case conferences on non-accidental injury to children in 1976.[4] The Maria Colwell scandal created a climate of opinion in which social workers were encouraged to be watchful and suspicious, and to remove children when in doubt; some departments took this policy much further than others. The new definition of child abuse probably helped social workers be more decisive; but it did not help them to offer sensitive assistance to well-motivated but overstressed parents.

Five years after the Maria Colwell tragedy, Jean Packman's research in a West-Country city found evidence that the new ideology of rescue was influencing every aspect of child-care practice in local authority social work.[5] She discovered that compulsory emergency removals of children from their families (Place of Safety Orders) were mooted in half of the cases where decisions were being made about whether or not to receive a child into care; and that they were used in one-third of those actually received into care. Compulsion was considered (and used) even when children or parents were requesting reception into care. Social workers were suspicious of voluntary agreements with parents to provide temporary care, and preferred care orders, which gave them 'more control'. 'Child abuse' was mentioned as an issue over the whole range of difficult children, and even in cases of adolescents where such violence as occurred was by child to parent.

The same trend towards court orders and compulsion is evident from national statistics of children in care. The total number of children in care on any day has steadily increased from just over 90,000 in 1972 to over 101,000 in 1977.[6] Annual admissions are not increasing, but children tend to stay in care longer; fewer return to parents, and more go out of care through reaching their eighteenth birthday.[7] The number of voluntary receptions into care under the 1948 Children Act fell from 43,500 in 1972 to 36,800 in 1977. Since these admissions tend to be short term, the proportion of children voluntarily in care on any one day (which used to stand at two-thirds or over) is now less than half; the other half are children on court orders.[8]

It is easy to understand why social workers, who have been accused by politicians and the Press of excessive permissiveness towards bad parents, should try to take decisive action, and seek the endorsement of a court order, to protect children from future changes of heart by parents or colleagues. However, compulsory orders, especially those involving emergency removal from home without preparation, inevitably polarise attitudes and jeopardise co-operation, at least in the short run. It is not surprising that Jean Packman found that some parents referred to social services staff as 'SS' or 'Nazis', and had little trust in them.[9]

(vi) Juvenile delinquency

A similar process of redefinition of social problems has occurred in the field of juvenile law-breaking. The aim of the 1969 Children and Young Persons Act, as it related to this problem, was to assimilate the services for young offenders into those for children in care – to integrate the depraved with the deprived, as some commentators put it. The intention was to reduce the numbers of children appearing before courts; to reduce compulsory orders for supervision, and use more voluntary agreements with social workers; to reduce court orders removing children from home, and substitute voluntary placements in the community; and, above all, to replace the old approved school orders with care orders, providing a flexible range of alternatives, with institutional placements as a reluctant last resort. The aim was also to provide a comprehensive counselling service to families with difficult children through the new social services departments, and a range of group activities which could be used – if necessary under court orders – to keep unruly children out of trouble. The 1969 Act aimed at redefining delinquency as being less a question of individual guilt and punishment, and more a matter of family adjustment and community responsibility.

In fact, research shows that what happened in the 1970s was almost exactly the opposite of what was intended. As the years went by, care orders were made on younger children with fewer previous offences.[10] Most of these found their way quickly into community schools – approved schools by new names. Within these schools, there was more emphasis on security, and a far higher proportion of such children found themselves under lock and key then had ever been thus restricted in the 1960s. Millham, Bullock and Hosie's researches show that the distinguishing feature of these children in secure units is not the degree of family disturbance or the number or seriousness of their previous offences – it is the number of unsuccessful placements they experienced in their earlier careers in public care.[11] Finally, many of these same children are hurried through the child-care system, and find themselves in detention centres, borstals, or on remand in prisons, before their sixteenth birthday. There are more children in these penal institutions than ever before – in spite of the attempt in the 1969 Act to abolish their use altogether for this age group.

This experience suggests that the version of paternalism applied to juvenile delinquency was particularly unsuccessful. In part this was a consequence of magistrates' mistrust of social workers and their recommendations, which may have encouraged the earlier use of penal orders. However, there is increasing evidence that social workers have been eager to use the provisions for supervision and care orders to deal with what they saw as potentially bad family situations, or potentially delinquent children. In one study, by Paley, Green and Thorpe, one-third of all care orders were made at children's first court appearances, mostly on social workers' recommendations.[12] Thus social workers' enthusiasm for the definition of delinquency as a form of maladjustment or family pathology often led to more drastic interventions – including removal from home – than the older approach (based on probation and the approved schools) would have prescribed.

So punitive have been the consequences of the 1969 Act that it is difficult to imagine how the notion that social workers are 'soft' with delinquents has survived. Yet the Conservatives have pledged to introduce new and tougher 'short sharp shocks' for vandals and hooligans. There are also moves afoot to restore the probation service to first place as the agency for juvenile supervision – a proposal aimed at promoting considerations of justice over welfare. It is ironical that such a measure might well *reduce* the numbers of children removed from home for offences, as 'welfare' has already become virtually synonymous with 'control'

(vii) Conclusions

An analysis of these fields of social services provision has shown that state officials have not served as an effective counterbalance to the ideologies of political leaders. Rather, they have reflected current political definitions of social problems and translated them into administrative rules and procedures. During the expansion of the social services, a paternalistic ideology justified many new white-collar posts, and an approach to social problems which mingled assistance with control, and disguised the nature of both. Since cuts in public expenditure began, rationing and suspicion of abuse have become more institutionalised in the agencies dispensing benefits, and overt control and punishment have emerged in many aspects of the social worker's role.

The new Conservatism takes these trends a stage further, and provides justifications for a much more abrasive and judgmental official style; conversely, it places no premium on compassion or sensitivity. Already there are signs that this new style is being taken up in the social services. For instance, to quote a local example, a series of letters to the journal *Social Work Today* by social workers from Exmouth, in Devon, have criticised left-wing permissiveness and welfare-rights activism as having encouraged irresponsibility among clients. A new group, 'Responsibility in Welfare', has been formed to promote 'conventional standards' in social work. Their spokesman, a divisional director of social services, commented in the local Press,[13]

> We also feel that social workers should only dispense welfare when they are certain that the person is making every effort to fend for himself. People can ask for more and more money from the state, saying they cannot cope on what they are given, but those are often the people who have colour television and continue to smoke and drink regularly.

Similarly, there have been few protests among social security staff about the cuts in discretionary payments to claimants of supplementary benefits. Staff have, through their unions, threatened to refuse to implement the Section which allows them to treat strikers' families as receiving £12 strike pay, even when they are receiving none. Here, the striker is perceived as a fellow-worker, and not strictly as a claimant; the cuts that affect claimants proper will apparently be quite cheerfully implemented.

Workers in the social services have put up more effective resistance to attempts to reduce their own numbers. However, this has been more a delaying action than a political victory — and, in the process of saving their own jobs, they have enforced lower standards of provision for their clients. It is thus to these consumers of the social services, increasingly rationed, harassed and controlled, that we should look for more angry resistance to the cuts in social expenditure under the new Conservative government.

Part 4

9 The new Conservatives and social policy

(i) The politics of class conflict

The new Conservative government took office armed with a radical zeal to change the face of economic and social policy in Britain. By the standards of recent years, the British economy was not in a state of crisis; but the new government insisted that it was suffering from the kind of long-term debility – a progressive illness, in fact – that required an immediate dose of its monetarist medicine. The illness was diagnosed in terms of the previous treatment that had been prescribed. Monetarist theory insisted that government had spent too much on bolstering up inefficient and unprofitable industry, through artificially inflated demand; and that governments had over-protected citizens through excessive spending on the social services. The only way to drive resources into the profitable channels that alone could produce an economic revival was to cut back all kinds of public spending, forcing both capital and labour out of the protected backwaters in which they have been stagnating.

There can be no doubt that the Conservatives were elected to do just these things. The British electorate had responded to their aggressive campaign against Labour's sluggish and complacent performance. The Callaghan government had attempted to justify its own monetarism in terms of the middle-ground consensus politics of the 1960s and early 1970s. It had explained public spending cuts and the compulsory restraint of pay in the public sector in much the same terms as Harold Wilson had always used – that industrial expansion was close at hand, and could be achieved if we all pulled together and tightened our belts for a time. The electorate quite rightly sensed that this was a distortion of the economic facts. It accurately perceived that

Callaghan consensus politics were false to the situation of 1979. It intuitively felt that Margaret Thatcher's politics of conflict and confrontation more accurately reflected the true issues of economic and social policy.

To understand why class conflict had become the political reality of the day we need to reconsider the 'Ricardo phenomenon'. Ricardo showed that while output is not expanding, and capitalists are using new machinery to save labour costs, the share of national income earned by labour must necessarily decline. He showed that under such circumstances as had prevailed in Britain throughout the 1970s, labour does not just *feel* that its economic situation is deteriorating through mechanisation; it actually is deteriorating. Labour is therefore likely to defend its position by fighting harder against capital – a fact reflected in Britain in the 1970s by increasingly lengthy and bitter strikes, and growing resistance against the closure of 'uneconomic' plant. So long as output does not expand to an extent which leads capital to reverse its policy of saving labour costs, this process must continue, and conflict must escalate, if labour is to act rationally, in its own interests.

The Heath government, after a brief period of confrontation, attempted to harmonise the two conflicting interests by Keynesian policies, aimed at producing political consensus. It increased employment directly, by employing more public servants; it gave direct assistance to ailing industries, thus saving jobs; and it put more money in the pockets of consumers through its fiscal policies. However, ultimately all the new money printed by the Heath government to finance these operations had to be spent on goods and services produced by private firms or the public corporations. The government's policies could only have succeeded in harmonising interests if decision-makers in these organisations had changed their plans, and decided to expand production of goods and services, and to use this new money to provide new employment as well as new machinery. This did not happen. Consequently the policies failed. The government had to go on borrowing more and more money to finance its programmes, and to support the poor and unemployed. The result was a rapid inflation, accompanied (after the oil crisis) by recession.

Thus the Labour government was forced to make an unpleasant choice. As redundancies grew in 1974 and 1975, it had to decide whether to tax producers more heavily, in order to make them pay more of the social costs of automation; or to cut public spending, in order to avoid the danger of industrial production falling still further. For to have raised taxation on producers would have been to risk further reductions in output, and even larger redundancies, whereas holding down state expenditure held out the prospect that in time the recession in industrial production could be reversed. The Labour government chose the second course, but in doing so it necessarily reinforced the deterioration in the economic position of workers and claimants. Consequently, this decision exacerbated the long-term conflict between the two interests.

Because the Labour government chose policies which strengthened the interests of capital, and worsened the situation of labour, it could never acknowledge that such a conflict of interests existed. It was forced to pursue policies which attacked the standards of living of workers and claimants, which led to high unemployment and growing poverty, while at the same time claiming to be acting in the interests of all citizens. The electorate was not deceived. However, since it had to rely on the Conservatives' version of the conflict that was taking place, it was forced to make a choice between the false consensus of Labour, or the strident conflict of the radical Right. It is probable that Labour's social policies were crucial in influencing that choice. The Callaghan government had consistently conveyed the message that public spending was too high, and that the social services (and their consumers) were an excessive burden on the productive sector of the economy. Yet under Labour, unemployment grew and the burden seemed ever to increase. Consequently, Margaret Thatcher's denunciations of the Welfare State and its beneficiaries were legitimated by Labour's own policies.

The Conservatives had no inhibitions about defining the economic situation in terms of conflict. They did not need to denounce the entire working class, but merely to attack the false leadership of those who promised growth of incomes without major change. Apart from the Callaghan government's dismal record, they could pick on union activists, especially in the public sector, and blame them for crippling the economy by demanding more and more of its life-blood. They argued that it was only an increase in profits that could produce the expansion of output necessary for higher incomes. This was not only consistent with the nineteenth-century model of economic growth that they espoused — it was also consistent with the policies that the Callaghan government had followed. No political group had attempted to convert the electorate to the notion that productive industry in

Britain had reached a stage of development in which it was unlikely ever again to require more workers, and very likely to require fewer and fewer. No politician tried to argue that, as a direct result of this, the state would have to transfer an ever-higher proportion of the national income to consumers, even to maintain their current standards of living. The only credible answer to the Conservative challenge was to answer fire with fire. The Conservatives were fighting for a larger share of national income for capital; the Labour government entirely failed to defend the interests of labour.

In the event, the consequences of Conservative policies have been far more disastrous than even the gloomiest economic forecasters predicted. The recession of 1980 is cutting far deeper into the incomes of workers than any previous post-war deflation. But the rapid decline in labour's fortunes is not a temporary feature, associated with the world economic climate. The Conservatives must necessarily (as was shown in Chapter 6) continue to try to force real wages down as part of their strategy for eventual growth. Having promised so much for the long term, and committed themselves so soon and so deeply to a radical version of their economic philosophy, Margaret Thatcher's ministers have no alternative but to see their policies through to the bitter end. At the time of writing, after eighteen months of Conservative government, it is becoming clearer every day, even to Thatcher's most ardent supporters, that the fall in the standards of living of British citizens is not a short-run stage in a race towards economic recovery. It is a necessary consequence of the combination of economic circumstances and government policies in Britain. National income will not expand in the foreseeable future; what is happening is that the majority of ordinary citizens are receiving smaller slices of a shrinking cake.

(ii) The attack on living standards

Social policies are an integral part of the Conservative economic strategy. The government justifies its approach to the needs of vulnerable minority groups in terms of the greatest good of the greatest number. Like the nineteenth-century political economists, it argues that attempts to give priority to protecting the weak from hardship will only impoverish the majority of citizens. In the long run, the standards of living of deprived people, like those of advantaged citizens, depend on prosperity and growth.

To achieve this requires major reductions in spending on social services in the short term. The Conservatives were already equipped with the means for achieving major cuts in local authority spending through the measures used by the Labour government. Throughout the 1970s, local government had become more and more dependent on central government to finance its expenditure. While local authority spending rose rapidly, especially under the Heath administration, the proportion of it paid for out of the local rates had declined from 39 per cent in 1965 to 27 per cent in 1975.[1] Labour had introduced a new principle in the grants made by central to local government — cash limits. The Conservatives had only to fix the total sums to be allocated to local authorities in order to achieve their objectives in this field of social services spending. Local government was left with the choice of how to implement the cuts, but not of whether to make them at all.

The radical innovation of Conservative social policy has been its determination to cut transfer payments. As we saw in Chapter 7, transfer payments alone among the three categories of social services spending had been increasing since 1975. By far the largest source of transfer spending is social security, which falls directly under central government control. In 1979, before the recession started to bite, social security spending already accounted for a quarter of all state expenditure. The Conservatives therefore embarked on a programme of reducing benefits.

This was a delicate operation, because of pledges that the Conservatives had given in opposition. They had consistently promised to maintain the standards of living of retirement pensioners. Since the rates of other National Insurance benefits were linked by law with the same indices as those of pensions, it was difficult to cut other benefits without making pensioners suffer. The Conservatives had also repeatedly promised to increase the value of child benefits before they came to power. This would obviously have expanded transfer payments.

Monetarist theorists have not always been opposed to transfer payments, as long as the principles behind them are simple. For instance, Milton Friedman has always advocated negative income tax, as a direct, labour-saving way of paying minimum incomes automatically to low-income families. As part of their critique of paternalism in social policy, the Conservatives had attacked the cumbersome complexity of the benefits system, and, in 1972, they had investigated a scheme for tax credits, similar to negative income tax. However, in office their urgent need to reduce public spending outweighed their theories about reforming the principles behind income maintenance schemes.

The Conservatives introduced three Social Security Bills in 1980, all producing cuts in benefits. They affected both National Insurance and supplementary benefits. In the first place, the link between the annual increase in benefits and the indices of prices and incomes was altered: benefits would rise with prices only. Second, earnings-related supplements to unemployment and sickness benefits were to be abolished, though this could not come into effect until 1981-2. It was also announced that the first eight weeks of sickness would not, in future, be covered by state benefits. The changes in supplementary benefits discussed in the previous two chapters were also introduced.

Because the rate of unemployment was increasing so rapidly during the summer of 1980 as a result of Conservative economic measures, these policies were clearly not going to reduce the total volume of state transfer spending in the foreseeable future; but they would diminish the size of what would otherwise have been an even larger expansion of transfers. They were also a direct attack on the standards of living of individual claimants of social security. Margaret Thatcher justified them by saying that all must expect to take their share of the hardship associated with change — as if unemployment itself was not an adequate form of suffering.

Yet these measures did not provoke much opposition. Inside Parliament there were predictable (and somewhat hypocritical) protests from Labour spokesmen, but outside there was little response from trade unionists. The working class had been very effectively divided by selectivist measures during the previous ten years. Workers resented the burden of taxation, and did not identify with social security claimants. Many workers subscribed to the right-wing ideology disseminated by the popular Press, suspecting the unemployed of 'scrounging' and dishonesty. Nothing that the Labour Party said or did when in office challenged these stereotypes; indeed, prejudices against state beneficiaries were reinforced by Labour's emphasis on social services spending as a burden on national resources. Hence it is not surprising that the Conservatives were able to implement these cuts without effective opposition.

This must have emboldened the Conservatives to consider more drastic measures. During 1980 there was a recommendation from the Rayner Committee (Sir Keith Joseph's Think Tank) that the government should consider merging unemployment and supplementary benefits. The most obvious economy measure implied by this change would be the total abolition of unemployment benefit. By making all the unemployed take a means test to establish eligibility for assistance, the Conservatives could defray an enormous proportion of the social security costs of their economic policies. Workers made redundant could be forced to spend their savings, to move into 'suitable' accommodation, and to adopt a life-style in keeping with their new status. The new supplementary benefits regulations would provide a far more inflexible approach to the needs of the newly unemployed, and allow the threat of benefit cuts to be used to drive claimants into low-wage employment. This would not only save money; it would be a far more abrasive style of dealing with unemployment – more in tune with the government's philosophy.

Conservative spokesmen close to Margaret Thatcher have for some time emphasised the importance of differentials between earnings and benefits, to provide a proper incentive for work. Since it is clearly an aim of Conservative economic policy to reduce wage levels (see Chapter 6), it is necessary for the government to consider ways of reducing benefit levels still further. The abolition of unemployment benefit would be far the most effective way of attacking the standards of living of the most rapidly rising sector of the population, and achieving this social policy aim.

(iii) Resisting the attack

As Conservative economic and social policies unfold, and reveal themselves as attempts to reduce the incomes of the working class, opposition to individual government measures will grow, and the groups formed to defend particular working-class interests will tend to coordinate with each other, and gradually to coalesce.

This will necessarily be a slow process, because the social and economic policies of previous governments have split the working class, not just between workers and claimants, but also between rival groups of workers. The promise that we can achieve economic growth by higher productivity has been held out to workers for so long that it will be difficult to alter the attitudes that accompanied it. Since the mid-1960s, workers have been indoctrinated with the idea that automation will necessarily produce more output, and hence higher incomes. Productivity deals have made this approach attractive, and have actually led to higher wages for some – at the expense of redundancy for others. Workers have been encouraged to see their colleagues as necessarily expendable in the cause of expanding incomes; the facts of the 'Ricardo phenomenon' have deliberately been obscured. Initially, each group will perceive the effects of Conservative measures only in terms of its narrow interests. Workers in high-technology employment may at first be beguiled by promises of long-term expansion; workers in low-paid employment may see the unemployed as the chief threat to their livelihood; and the unemployed themselves may be as bitter against their colleagues in employment as against the government.

Yet the evidence of the 1930s suggests that eventually the working class will tend to unite against the kind of measures that the Conservatives are adopting. Throughout the 1920s, with 1 million or more unemployed, the labour movement remained relatively passive and complacent about unemployment. The Communist-inspired – but very independent – National Unemployed Workers Movement (NUWM) organised protests and marches against policies which harmed the unemployed or increased their numbers. The famous 'Hunger Marches' took place every four years throughout the 1920s, and the NUWM campaigned against cuts in wages or the dole, using the slogan 'Work at trade union rates or full maintenance.' But although the trade unions had struggles of their own throughout this period in defence of their members' living standards, employed workers and the unemployed were not effectively united, and the unemployed remained isolated and vulnerable, as well as ineffective in support of their colleagues in work.

In 1931, at the time of the great economic and political crisis of the Labour government, the May Committee recommended a 20 per cent reduction in the rates of unemployment benefit as one of the measures to balance the Budget. This caused a split in the Cabinet, and was one of the factors in Macdonald's secession to form a National Government. But when cuts in the dole were actually made, the reaction outside government and parliament was not particularly fierce or united. It was not until the summer of the following year that, quite suddenly, the labour movement started to rally and unite. During the Hunger March of 1932, several leaders were arrested and imprisoned under a statute of Edward II, which caused a national uproar. In September, the government attempted to apply means tests to the dole (transitional benefits). In Birkenhead, there was prolonged rioting and clashes between police and demonstrators representing the NUWM and trade unionists. Many Labour-controlled local authorities, which were supposed to introduce the means test, refused to do so, and were taken over by government commissioners. In April 1934, after persistent pressure by the NUWM, with solid trade union support and growing public protest, the standard rates of unemployment benefit, cut in 1931, were restored. In 1935, the newly created Unemployment Assistance Board — which had replaced the troublesome local authority committees in the task of dealing with the unemployed — tried to introduce a harsher test of means, with reductions in scales of assistance. The reaction in the labour movement was[2]

immediate and sustained in every sector. The anthracite miners called a twenty-four hour protest strike. The South Wales Miners' Federation called an All-Wales conference and set up a council of action. In that area, 300,000 people demonstrated. In Scotland and on Tyneside, as in South Wales, protesting women smashed the windows and sometimes stoned the doorways of the U.A.B. offices. Protests came not only from innumerable individual borough councillors and county councillors but from whole county councils and local authorities speaking as elected bodies. Groups of doctors protested, religious organisations of all denominations protested. And many local Labour parties joined with the Communists in protest.

The government quickly announced that the previous scales would be restored.

It would appear that in the 1930s the unemployed provided a great deal of the spontaneous (and often violent) resistance to government cutbacks, while the trade unions provided the mass support, and the political leadership to capitalise on the effects of direct action. Although the unemployed were very well organised in many areas through the NUWM, this was mainly for day-to-day solidarity and support. It seems unlikely that the main body of the Birkenhead rioters or the Welsh stone-throwers were in fact members of any organisation. More probably they were disorganised groups of unemployed people and their families, frustrated beyond endurance at the treatment they had received from the authorities. In this sense, really effective protest required both highly inflammable groups to produce the initial explosion, and a more solid mass to follow it up. The spark cannot really be anticipated; the combustive material cannot really be collected or directed. What can be organised is the co-ordinated support when such a spontaneous outbreak of resistance occurs.

It is very difficult to anticipate the point at which parallel violence and mass resistance in the face of Conservative measures might take place in the 1980s. At the time of writing (summer 1980), there is no real evidence either of spontaneous rebellion by claimants, or of organised support by trade unionists; but none of the cuts in social security benefits have yet come into effect. Already an all-party group of MPs, the majority of whom were Conservatives, have warned of public disorder in Wales if unemployment goes on rising.[3] In 1981, when there are likely to be between 2 and 3 million unemployed, and the government will probably be several stages further on in its programme of cuts, the picture may be changing fairly rapidly. Already in 1980, the trade union movement is moving to reassess its attitudes towards unemployment and the unemployed. At a conference organised by the Liverpool Trades Council in April 1980, a series of speakers attacked productivity-dealing and the exclusion of the unemployed from membership of and participation in trade unions. The conference was aptly called 'Not Back to the 1930's'; yet it might well presage a return to the solidarity and organised resistance of that decade.

It is interesting that in all the riots over the reduced scales of assistance in the 1930s, the active and violent role of women was reported. Women undoubtedly play a vital role in determining the effectiveness of direct action in the labour movement. When wives support their husbands in a strike, it is very much more likely to endure to a successful conclusion. When government measures attack the standards of living of wage-earners or state beneficiaries, women are always the hardest hit, both as low-wage workers and as wives. Perhaps, also, they play an important role in creating either division or unity between different groups of workers and claimants. It may be that in the 1980s, only when women unite in protest against Conservative attacks on the standard of living of the working class will the labour movement achieve the solidarity necessary for effective resistance.

Hitherto, trade unionists have concentrated most of their protest on the Conservatives' plans for legislating against effective union organisation during strikes. But the government has, with characteristic abrasiveness, drawn attention to the links between its policies over social security and those over industrial relations by insisting on reductions in the supplementary benefit paid to strikers' families. This is precisely the sort of issue around which links between the divided sections of the working class can be made. As trade unionists become more acquainted with the realities of life on social security, they will be less hasty in their condemnation of the unemployed. Equally, many claimants who have been driven into a twilight world of petty crime and fraud, and into seeking casual work to evade the benefit authorities' scrutiny, will for the first time see a positive interest in their situation by trade unions. The present government's cuts are far harsher in their effects than were those of the National Government in the early 1930s; they may therefore serve to reunite a working class that has been more deeply divided by the social policies of the 1970s.

(iv) Conclusions

As the number of unemployed in Britain approached 2 million in July 1980, Margaret Thatcher announced that the government would not change its policies because 'there are no U-turns available.' The phrase conjured up a rather vivid image of the government hurtling down a motorway with a barricaded central reservation. She might have added that there were no charted exits either, for quite some distance ahead.

In the first Budget after it took office, the Conservative government had announced fiscal measures which raised the annual rate of inflation to near 20 per cent, soon after it had fallen into single figures for the first time for five years. This had really committed the government to pursuing its own remedies for inflation far more zealously than would otherwise have been necessary. For all the reasons examined in this book, the remedies were both ineffective and destructive. However, this government, unlike its predecessors, was committed to a course of action from which it could not retreat. As its first round of policies fail, it is driven to looking for new and more drastic measures along the same policy lines.

One of its highest priorities was to reduce the Public Sector Borrowing Requirement. But mainly because of the enormous extra cost of unemployment benefit, and the government's determination to increase defence expenditure, there are forecasts that the PSBR may be as much as twice as high as the government's target. Furthermore, the private sector is looking to borrow more because of its cash-flow problems. Consequently, the whole monetarist strategy is under threat. The government is having to consider alternative means of keeping down public spending in order to check the growth in the money supply.

The most immediate method the government has already used, and could employ to a greater extent, is the sale of public sector assets. Having already disposed of the profitable parts of a number of nationalised industries, it could quickly identify others and sell them off. (Its enthusiasm is unlikely to match that of some Conservative local councils, such as Torbay, which put its potentially profitable public lavatories up for sale.)

For the longer term, however, the government must look to the social services for further savings. If it relieved the local authorities of their duties to provide certain services (accommodation for the homeless, aid to the chronically sick and disabled, for instance) it could argue for still stricter cash limits, and cuts in such capital expenditure programmes as still exist. Even more inviting is the prospect of holding down social security benefits below the level of the rise in prices, which could save more than any other single cut available.

However, the most ideologically appealing of the options is the abolition of unemployment benefit. If the Conservatives took this step, it would be a direct reference back to the 1930s, for it would reflect exactly the issue that united the working class in that era — the application of a means test to a far larger proportion of the unemployed, and the consequent exclusion of a high proportion of better-paid workers from benefit. As redundancies continue to grow, the prospect of unemployment will become far more real to those who had previously seen it as something that happened to the unskilled and undeserving, and the trade unions will be forced into taking a far more active part in campaigns against social security cuts. Thus the future of unemployment benefit is a key issue in the growing conflict between the government and the working class.

In the long run, though, resistance to such measures is not a sufficient strategy for the labour movement. It must reconsider its whole stance on economic growth, on productivity, and on the role of government in maintaining income for consumption. The Conservatives' efforts to reduce transfer spending serve to focus attention on that role. But at present there is an ideological vacuum in the labour movement on this issue. No coherent account of the importance of transfer payments exists to serve in a positive programme for social policy. It is this question which requires attention in the final chapter.

10 Alternative futures

(i) Growth and conflict

My purpose in this book has been to reanalyse the issue of economic growth in advanced industrial nations, and to point out some of its limits and costs. I have shown that automation which produces higher output per person employed in productive industry does not necessarily increase national income, and that when it does not, it reduces the incomes of the working class. I have suggested that some such point will be reached in every advanced industrialised country eventually. Britain, as the first nation to mechanise production, is merely experiencing the first example of a universal phenomenon of technological change. It is having the first glimpse of the true nature of automation — the replacement of human workers by machines, and the transition from a hand-made to a machine-made economy.

The final questions to be discussed in this book are the political implications of these radical economic changes. Political life in all post-war Western countries has been dominated by the priority of increasing national income. This priority has tended to produce social democratic governments, which appealed to a consensus of class interests in the name of national prosperity. Such governments have argued that the only way in which all can be better off is for the national economy to grow. Social services have also been expanded, often faster than the rate of growth of GDP, but the purpose of this extra social expenditure was to compensate individuals and families who could not share in rising national prosperity. The expansion of social services expenditure has been made conditional on the growth of the economy as a whole.

During this era, countries like Japan were held up as examples of success by more conservative governments, because Japan has had very rapid growth with very low rates of *state* spending on its social services. Countries like West Germany and Sweden were chosen as examples by governments more conscious of social issues, because they have devoted a fairly high proportion of national income to social services, but still had a high rate of growth. Throughout this book I have argued that there is an alternative to economic growth as a means of improving the quality of life of all citizens; and that this is the *only* way of achieving that end once the process of automation begins to replace workers without increasing output. The alternative consists in using the higher productivity provided by new technology to give more *leisure* for all, at the same total income.

This is because the very nature of automation at this stage of the process of industrialisation is different from the nature of mechanisation at an earlier stage. During the stage of mechanisation, higher output is achieved at the same cost by the use of more machinery and the same amount of labour. During the stage of automation, the same output is achieved at lower cost, by using more technology and less human labour. (Nineteenth-century political economists – especially Mill – anticipated some such development in their concept of the 'stationary state'.) Consequently, in the present stage of economic change in Britain, what is produced is not more output but more leisure.

However, if governments continue to attempt to achieve higher national income, it is in the nature of this stage of development that the result will merely be a fall in the incomes of the working class. Indeed, this consequence is inevitable unless the power of the state is used in the opposite direction, to give more income to workers no longer required by productive industry. Thus the policies required to maintain living standards during the stage of automation are entirely different from the policies that could be followed during the stage of mechanisation.

Indeed, the economic and social policies required by the alternative to economic growth are not consistent with the social democratic politics of consensus. The alternative requires a government willing to challenge the interests of the owners of the means of production in the name of the living standards of the working class.

Since the Second World War, Keynesian economic policies have seemed to provide Western governments with a permanent rationale for supporting the continued expansion of private productive industry, often using public resources to that end. In the 1960s Galbraith showed in *The New Industrial State* that private and public capital were tending to merge, because major projects based on advanced technology involved such high costs and long-term planning.

However, as I showed in the previous chapter, by the mid-1970s in Britain, government could no longer honestly argue that its support for the growth of productive industry was increasing the incomes of the working class. Because of the 'Ricardo phenomenon', productive industry was using any increase in profits to accelerate automation and redundancy, and reduce labour costs. State investment in high-technology projects like nuclear power and Concorde was using revenue from taxes on workers to finance programmes which distributed far less than these sums in wages to their employees. Hence, the Labour government was forced to choose between continuing to represent the situation in terms of a false consensus of interests, while actually reinforcing a fall in the living standards of the working class; or challenging this trend by using the power of the state against the owners of the means of production. It chose the former course.

Because of the 'Ricardo phenomenon', there is now in Britain a conflict of interests between capital and labour, and the Conservative government's policies merely give expression to that conflict. These same policies must serve to unite the labour movement, which has been divided both by the economics of new technology and productivity, and the politics of paternalism. Political groups on the Left may disagree about the nature of the 'crisis of capitalism', the necessary conditions for change, and the priorities in an alternative society. But they will tend to be drawn together in resistance against Conservative measures. Above all, they will perceive, as ordinary working-class people must increasingly perceive, that the forces of capitalism are being deployed to drive down their incomes.

(ii) Ricardo and Marx

An important source of theoretical consensus in the labour movement might arise from the application of Marxist theory to the present situation in Britain. In Chapter 1, we saw that Ricardo both identified the circumstances in which the share of national income consumed by the working class would shrink as a result of technological change, and argued that certain economic conditions would prevent these circumstances from arising, other than over short periods. Marx, however, in his critique of political economy, took the opposite stand. He argued that there was a constant 'struggle between the worker and the machine',[1] because 'the productivity of a machine is ... measured by the extent to which it replaced human labour power.'[2] Hence, under capitalism, the interests of workers were perpetually opposed to the mechanisation of industrial production. He quoted with approval Ricardo's recognition of the short-term damage to workers' incomes done by rapid technological change, but went on to claim that there could be no long-term 'compensation' in terms of new employment for redundant workers.

Marx's analysis was complex, and any summary of it is necessarily an oversimplification. He argued that capital accumulation occurred through the extraction by the capitalist of surplus labour value — that profits were, in effect, the result of unpaid work by employees. As industrialisation proceeded, and more complex machinery was introduced, this gradually replaced labour power through the process of capital accumulation based on surplus value. Marx saw this as in itself implying that a diminishing share of national income went to workers. Real wages could only rise as a short-term phenomenon, associated with a temporary scarcity of labour. In the long run, however,[3]

in proportion as capital accumulates, the condition of the worker, be his wages high or low, necessarily grows worse. ... The accumulation of wealth at one pole of society involves a simultaneous accumulation of poverty, labour torment, slavery, ignorance, brutalisation, and moral degradation, at the opposite pole.

Marx rejected Ricardo's assumptions about the probability of conditions leading to long-term growth in real wages. He thought that new technology 'necessarily displaces workers in the branches of industry into which it is introduced.'[4] He recognised that the same process might 'none the less lead to an increase in employment in other branches of industry,'[5] but only as a result of an increased demand for raw materials, or for the product itself — if it was used as a material for some other product — because it was more cheaply supplied. However, each of these earlier or later processes would eventually be mechanised, displacing these additional workers. Ultimately, the only class to gain by new technology would be 'the capitalist class and its hangers on'. Mechanisation 'greatly enlarges these social strata.'[6]

Gradually, skilled workers would be replaced by machines, and the only employment to increase would be unproductive work, and particularly domestic service:[7]

> All the persons employed in textile factories and in mines taken together number 1,208,442; those employed in textile factories and metal industries taken together number 1,039,605 — in either case less than the number of modern domestic slaves. What an edifying result of the capitalist exploitation of machinery!

Yet these same domestic servants, and the surplus rural labour of the period, provided much of the labour that continued to migrate from low-productivity to new higher-productivity industrial employment in the last quarter of the nineteenth century, and the first decade of the twentieth. Ricardo's optimism seemed to some extent justified by the progress of industrialisation and the rise in real wages, even after Britain achieved its peak share of world trade, and began to decline as an exporting nation. Despite Marx's fulminations against 'the so-called theory of compensation', new industries based on new technology did arise, and produce new products (motor cars, electrical goods). The oldest-established industrial areas of the North did indeed suffer, from trade cycles and from displacement of labour by new processes, exactly as Marx predicted; but in other areas new factories sprang up, and workers grew affluent. Marxists began to modify his theories, or emphasise other aspects of them.

Yet since the mid-1960s in Britain, Marx's notion of displacement of labour, and the effects of capital accumulation, have been directly applicable. As capital has expanded, the demand for labour[8]

> declines relative to the magnitude of total capital, and at an accelerated rate, as this magnitude increases. With the growth of total capital, . . . the labour incorporated in it does also increase; but in a constantly diminishing proportion . . . in fact, . . . capitalist accumulation itself . . . constantly produces, and produces in direct proportion to its energy and extent, a relatively redundant population of workers.

As Marx suggested, new technology does not, under capitalism, lead to a more leisured society, but to a more unequal one.[9]

The law in accordance with which a continually increasing quantity of the means of production can, thanks to the advance in productivity of social labour, be set in motion by a progressively diminishing expenditure on human energy – this law, in a capitalist society (where the worker does not make use of the means of production, but where the means of production make use of the worker), undergoes a complete inversion, and is expressed as follows: the higher the productivity of labour, the greater is the pressure of the workers on the means of employment; and the more precarious, therefore, becomes their condition of existence. . . . Under capitalism, likewise, the fact that the means of production and the productivity of labour grow more rapidly than does the productive population, secures expression in an inverse way, namely that the working population always grows more quickly than capital's need for self-expansion.

Finally, Marx predicted the growth of a semi-employed category of workers, receiving very low wages for occasional work, and an increase in the number of people dependent on the Poor Law – he called the former 'the industrial reserve army', and the latter 'paupers':[10]

the larger the reserve army as compared with the active labour army, the larger is the mass of the consolidated surplus population, whose poverty is in inverse ratio to its torment of labour . . . and the larger the industrial reserve army, the larger, too, is the army of those who are officially accounted paupers.

Thus, the stage of its economic development reached by Britain in the 1970s has come to reflect – one hundred years after he first outlined it – precisely the picture of advanced industrialisation that Marx painted. There are several ironies in this historical coincidence. Ricardo's theory of economic growth and technological change held sway throughout the nineteenth century, despite Marx's criticisms. In the twentieth century, many non-industrialised countries adopted Marxist approaches to economic development, while industrialised nations modified Ricardo under the influence of Keynes. Marx agreed with only one chapter of Ricardo's book – the one entitled 'On Machinery', upon which he drew extensively for his theory, and generalised far beyond Ricardo's intentions. In 1979, the British government

finally rejected Keynes and all his works, and returned to an unmodi-
fied version of Ricardo's theory of growth — to a philosophy of un-
restrained capitalism and competition. Yet it did so under precisely
the conditions that Ricardo stipulated as destructive of the liveli-
hoods of the working class. I have argued that these conditions are
now long-term ones, and that Britain's stage of industrial development entails that they will continue for the foreseeable future. Hence,
Marx's careful analysis of mechanisation and the automation of production — of the true nature of the technological changes Ricardo
first incorporated into economic theory — at last becomes, as Marx
would have put it, 'the absolute general law of capitalist accumulation'.

The crux of Marx's theory was that the worker, who had only his
labour power to sell, was ultimately vulnerable to the machine. Marx
repeatedly gave examples of how new technology replaced skilled
workmen by machines, and quoted capitalists who stated that their
purpose was precisely to do this, and to save labour costs. He argued
that women and children would find more employment, and skilled
men less, as automatic methods of production advanced. He would
have used examples today from the field of microelectronics, where
many of the areas of greatest expansion of production — Brazil,
Taiwan — have no strong tradition of skills, but an abundant supply
of cheap labour. Now that the stage of automation has been reached
in the British economy, Ricardo's theory of compensatory employment in new industry no longer applies, and Marx's analysis of the
antagonism between worker and machine becomes the dominant
principle.

It is not the purpose of this book to analyse in any detail how the
radical alternatives to recent economic and social policies might be
implemented. Everything that I have written in earlier chapters has
indicated the confusion and irrelevance of the Labour Party and trade
union leadership in the face of the central issues of recent political
struggles, and, above all, in the class struggle that is now in progress.
As the Conservative government implements the new politics of confrontation, the labour movement must necessarily coalesce in new
configurations, which reflect a more effectively organised resistance.

The first manifestations of these changes were becoming visible
in the Labour Party in 1980. James Callaghan's leadership was challenged by the Left, and he resigned; a group of right-wing ex-ministers
was openly threatening to leave the party, possibly to join a new
Centre coalition, if its policies do not remain dominant. These ministers

are without deep roots or extensive support in the party or the labour movement. However, the ascendancy of the 'moderate' leadership of the Labour Party appears likely to continue to be guaranteed by the traditional leadership of the largest trade unions. Hence, it seems unlikely that the Labour Party will adopt policies relevant to the class struggle now in progress – at least until after it loses the next general election. Then the Labour Party will be in disarray, and many things might happen. I would not rule out the possibility that the Labour Party, as the traditional vehicle of working-class political action, could then, after a major upheaval from the grass roots of the labour movement, fall into the hands of an entirely new leadership that would adopt policies relevant to the economic and social realities of the 1980s.

I shall not attempt to speculate about the appropriate political tactics to be adopted by such a leadership, or the measures that might be necessary for it to govern effectively. It was, of course, a central part of Marx's argument that the capitalist accumulation in which automation was the final stage must always and necessarily be against the interests of workers, and that only revolutionary change, through the power of the state, could reverse the oppressive logic of competition and profit. It follows from this that only the socialisation of the means of production could turn automation into a benign and leisure-giving process.

None the less, it seems to me worth considering how in theory this might be achieved, without anticipating the political means of accomplishing it. Given that Britain is part of a competitive world economy, and has little or no chance of improving its trading position, how might we improve the living standards of our citizens?

The first unavoidable fact that has to be taken into consideration is that technological change means that the same amount of goods can be produced for less labour, and that, consequently, if automation is allowed to proceed, the wages of productive labour must continue to fall. The second unavoidable fact is that Britain is a small island that cannot feed itself, and consequently has to live by exporting. Unless technological progress does continue, British manufactured goods must necessarily become more expensive than those of Britain's industrial competitors. Assuming constant output, therefore, the share of national income going to wages must diminish.

It follows that the only guarantee of the living standards of all citizens lies in the power of the state to alter the social consequences of automation, and create an entirely different social order. We have seen that under capitalism there are three distinct consequences of the 'Ricardo phenomenon'. The first is that the state itself grows, expanding its activity on behalf of the dominant social order, and particularly increasing its role in social control. Second, there is a growth in the wealth and power of business corporations, and in the professional and financial sectors. Institutions which own the machinery that replaces labour, or finance its introduction, must necessarily, as the share of wages in national income falls, increase their share. Third, there is an increase in transfer payments to displaced workers, though its size depends upon the ruthlessness of the government in power.

If we accept Marx's argument that all the income that goes towards automation is simply surplus labour value, the problem of a socialist government would be to ensure that enough of this income was actually spent on machinery that would reduce the volume and unpleasantness of work, and that workers would receive adequate compensation for their *past* labour (and that of their parents and more distant ancestors) which alone provided this machinery. A socialist government would seek to ensure that this surplus labour value was not spent on the socially wasteful proliferation either of state employment and remuneration, or of employment of personnel in the superstructure of the industrial and financial worlds. It would define as an important part of its role the payment of an adequate weekly income for life to workers displaced by machinery.

At present, there are no such principles behind the growth of the state and industrial superstructure, or the compensation of displaced workers. The capitalist economy has produced a social order in which much meaningless and unnecessary work is done, and much that is actually socially harmful and destructive. Yet every citizen is supposed to evaluate his fellow-citizens in terms of the incomes they earn, and to despise those who have been displaced by automation, and cannot find employment. A socialist government would need to create a society in which these attitudes were challenged by the realities of everyday life.

(iii) The social dividend

One important change that workers could immediately adopt is the rejection of productivity-dealing as it is at present conceived. Instead of negotiating for higher wages for a reduced workforce, unions could negotiate for a shorter working week for the same number of employees – or even for more.

Employers have consistently rejected the shorter working week in productive industry, insisting that the economics of mechanical production require that plant is operated for twenty-four hours a day. However, there is no good reason why three, or even four, shifts should not replace the traditional day and night shift arrangement in industry. This would ensure that a higher number of workers were employed, even as automation progressed.

However, it would also mean that wages fell, for it is of the very nature of automation that, unless output increases, the wage bill must fall. This has been happening for fifteen years in productive industry, but workers have been blinded to it by the fact that the brunt of its impact has been felt by those displaced as redundant, and school-leavers who have been unable to find employment. Hence it would only be by negotiating for a shorter working week, and forgoing both productivity-dealing and overtime payments, that workers could experience the reality of the effects of automation on the incomes of the whole of their class.

If they did so, they would immediately perceive the need to improve the 'social wage'. Instead of resenting the role of the state in transferring income through taxation, they would see that this was a necessary part of the process of automation. For only by increasing that part of the income of wage- and salary-earners paid for out of the benefits of automation can the standards of living of this sector be maintained or improved. They would also see that it was from their labour that the income to instal new machinery was produced, and that therefore social justice demanded this compensation.

The notion which most clearly expresses this role of the state is that of the 'social dividend'. This term was invented by Major C.H. Douglas, the unorthodox economist of the 1920s. Douglas grasped the implications of new technology without perceiving the economic limitations on growth. He thought that automation could guarantee unlimited growth for any industrial nation, based simply on the potentialities of scientific invention and its application. He considered that, irrespective of international competition, Britain had merely to expand output, and pay every citizen a higher income through the state in measure with this expansion. The first notion was unrealistically optimistic; the second was a sound step toward social justice.

If output remains static for the reasons given in the first chapter, the measure of the appropriate increase in the social dividend is the growth of automation. As the value of new machinery increases, and labour costs are saved, so should the weekly amounts paid by the state to all those who have only their labour power to sell. The only sound principle on which to achieve this is the universal distribution of a weekly social dividend to be paid to all citizens. The dividend would be raised by taxation on the owners of the means of production or, if they were in state ownership, by measure with the growth of the means of production.

This would entail that, as automation progressed, state benefits would gradually replace earnings from wages and salaries, at exactly the same rate as machines replaced workers. At present, transfer payments are increasing with automation, as we saw in Chapter 2. But the trend in this direction is reluctant and accompanied by much resentment and stigma; and the burden of raising the revenue for these transfers falls mainly on the wages and salaries of workers. If we conceive of automation as the result of the labour of past generations of workers, and of those recently employed, then the social dividend has truly been earned, and is not 'something for nothing'. Equally, if we see it as compensation for the falling levels of total wages which are inevitable in automation, it is clearly the only socially just way of dealing with the consequences of new technology.

There are many alternative methods of introducing a social dividend. However, it could be done quite simply, using the structure of present social security benefits. Initially, child benefits (the allowances which most resemble a social dividend in their structure) could be increased regularly and substantially every year. This would serve a number of purposes. For many years, Britain has lagged behind its European neighbours in these payments. Families with children, both in and out of work, are the most poverty-stricken in the country. Substantial increases in child benefits would compensate families for the decline in their relative standards of living; it would also help many single parents come off supplementary benefits. Above all, it would help establish the principle, in a recognisable, familiar form, of benefits paid universally and unconditionally to all citizens, irrespective of whether or not they were in employment.

Second, the state could guarantee a weekly, non-means-tested income to the unemployed and single parents, by extending unemployment benefits, and adopting a guaranteed maintenance allowance. In this way, the stigma of full dependence on the state would be removed, and the punitive trend of recent social policy would be reversed.

Once these two steps were taken, the state could start introducing a universal weekly benefit, paid to all citizens, which would increase annually with the growth of automated methods of production. This would provide workers with the incentive to co-operate with new technology, knowing that it did not represent an attack on their standards of living, and that they would benefit in leisure and ease of life from its introduction, even if output did not increase.

We know from the experience of recent years that productivity can be improved, and labour costs saved, without significant increases in the volume of investment or profit. Innovation and the application of new technology are sufficient to guarantee considerable improvements in these directions. Thus even though the silicon chip and other microelectronic processes will make many more workers redundant, they will also lower costs and improve efficiency. So long as the consequent savings are used for socially useful products, and workers displaced are paid a social dividend, the results of technological change can be made benign, through the power of the state.

(iv) Other alternatives

I have suggested that this active role for the state is very unlikely to come into existence without bitter conflict, but that such conflict, on class lines, is inevitable in any case. The only other way in which capitalist economies have resolved the kind of situation that exists in Britain today is through wars.

Many of the features of the 'Ricardo phenomenon' were present in the British economy in the 1920s and 1930s. National product grew by only 10 per cent between 1920 and 1932, in spite of an increase in fixed capital formation of over 60 per cent.[11] Output per worker increased by 22 per cent in the same twelve years,[12] but income from wages actually declined, as did personal disposable income *per capita*.[13] In other words, there was the same combination of rapid technological change, rising productivity, high unemployment, stagnant output, and falling real incomes as exist today. Rearmament contributed substantially to the partial recovery of the later 1930s, but it was only during the war that full employment was achieved − in 1938 there were still over 2 million unemployed. The Conservative government is already increasing expenditure on 'defence', and adopting some intransigent stances in foreign affairs. The temptation to try to solve Britain's economic problems in those directions will increase with the failure of monetarist policies, and the rise in domestic strife and violence.

(v) Conclusion

To many readers, this may seem a very gloomy conclusion; to others, my analysis of the probable development of a greater class-consciousness and cohesion in the working class may seem to offer more hope. I am not suggesting that these events will simply take their course, or that one outcome is already predetermined and inevitable. On the contrary, the struggles of every individual and group will contribute to the eventual outcome, which is at present highly uncertain. We are in a period of rapid change, which is a transition − in one direction or another − to a different kind of society. Change is taking place at every level of the structure, and every one of us is directly involved in it.

For instance, in Chapter 8 I analysed the role of social workers and other Welfare State officials in the evolution of social policy. I argued that, when an overview of the consequence of social policy changes was taken, they seemed to have played a rather passive role, and exerted little influence. However, running counter to this tide of official collusion with political definitions of social problems has been a strong undercurrent of resistance among workers in the Welfare State. As conflict sharpens along class lines, and issues become clearer, there will be a role for such workers in raising the consciousness of their clients, and making links with other organisations of resistance.

My analysis points clearly to one conclusion. This is that rapid economic growth is very unlikely to occur again in Britain, under peacetime conditions, and that automation of production is bound to continue if we are to remain competitive in the world economy. In spite of the inevitable reductions in employment and incomes from wages that this will entail, a better and freer life for all is possible. However, this will not occur under the kind of capitalist political economy that is the basis of our present society. Only far deeper and broader changes in the structure of our society can bring it about.

Notes

1 The problem of economic growth

1 Central Statistical Office, *Annual Abstract of Statistics, 1980*, HMSO, 1980, Table 6.1; and Department of Employment, *Employment Gazette*, vol. 88, no. 6, June 1980, p. 655.
2 Central Statistical Office, *Annual Abstract of Statistics*, op. cit., Table 6.1.
3 Ibid.
4 Ibid.
5 Central Statistical Office, *National Income and Expenditure*, HMSO, 1979, Table 7.2.
6 Department of Employment, *British Labour Statistics, Year Book 1976*, HMSO, 1978, Table 156; and *Employment Gazette*, vol. 88, no. 6, June 1980, p. 710.
7 Robert Bacon and Walter Eltis, *Britain's Economic Problem: Too Few Producers*, 2nd edn, Macmillan, 1978, p. 7.
8 Central Statistical Office, *National Income and Expenditure*, op. cit., Table 1.3, using implied deflator for income from employment, Table 2.5.
9 Department of Employment, *British Labour Statistics, Year Book 1976*, op. cit., Table 21; and *Employment Gazette*, vol. 88, no. 6, June 1980, p. 695. *National Income and Expenditure*, op. cit., Table 1.3, using implied deflator for consumers' expenditure, Table 2.5.
10 Department of Employment, *British Labour Statistics, Year Book 1976*, op. cit., Table 156; and *Employment Gazette*, vol. 88, no. 4, April 1980, p. 454.
11 *Employment Gazette*, April 1980, op. cit., p. 454.
12 Bacon and Eltis, op. cit., p. 208.
13 Ibid., p. 209.
14 Ibid., p. 213.
15 David Hume, 'A Treatise on Money', in E. Rotwein, ed., *David Hume, Writings on Economics*, Nelson, 1955.

16 Milton Friedman, *Dollars and Deficits: Inflation, Monetary Policy and the Balance of Payments*, Prentice Hall, 1968, pp. 25-6.
17 J.K. Galbraith, *Money, Whence it Came, Where it Went*, Deutsch, 1975, pp. 90-100.
18 David Ricardo, *Principles of Political Economy and Taxation* (1817), Everyman Edition, Dent, 1912, p. 264.
19 Ibid., p. 264.
20 Ibid., p. 267.
21 Ibid., p. 267.
22 Ibid., p. 270.
23 J. Walker, *British Economic and Social History, 1700-1977*, 2nd edn, MacDonald & Evans, 1979, p. 271.
24 Ibid., p. 277.
25 Ibid., p. 323; and 'Britain Cottons on to Chaos', the *Guardian*, 16 June 1980.
26 Ibid.
27 J.S. Mill, *The Principles of Political Economy, with Some of their Applications to Social Philosophy* (1848), Longmans, 1891, p. 454.
28 J.H. Clapham, *The Economic Development of France and Germany, 1915-1914* (1921), 4th edn, Cambridge University Press, 1948, p. 5.
29 Ibid., p. 53.
30 Ibid., p. 278.
31 Bacon and Eltis, op. cit., pp. 147, 213.
32 M. Collins, *L'Economie politique, source des revolutions et des utopies pretendues socialistes*, Paris, 1857, vol. III, p. 331.
33 Bacon and Eltis, op. cit., p. 9.
34 Ibid., p. 20.
35 Ibid., pp. 24, 28.
36 Ibid., pp. 210, 150, 152, 208.
37 Ibid., p. 213.
38 Ibid., pp. 214, 213, 210.
39 Ibid., pp. 213, 208.
40 Central Statistics Office, *Statistical Abstract of Ireland, 1977*, Stationery Office, 1980, p. 63.
41 Ibid., Table 107.
42 Ibid., Table 231.
43 Ibid., p. 238.
44 Ibid., Table 140.
45 *The Financial Times*, 29 July 1980.

2 Social consequences of the problem

1 J.S. Mill, *The Principles of Political Economy, with Some of their Applications to Social Philosophy* (1848), Longmans, 1891.
2 M. Friedman, *There's No Such Thing as a Free Lunch*, Open Court, 1975, p. 116.

3   B. Abel-Smith, *Labour's Social Plans*, Fabian Tract 369, Fabian
    Society, 1966, p. 9.
4   I. Gough, *The Political Economy of the Welfare State*, Macmillan,
    1979, p. 79.
5   Department of Employment, *British Labour Statistics, Year Book
    1976*, HMSO, 1978, Table 130; and *Family Expenditure Survey,
    1979*.
6   David Cockcroft, quoted in Mary Goldring, 'Into the Electronic
    80's', *The Listener*, 24 May 1979.
7   Department of Health and Social Security, *Social Assistance: A
    Review of the Supplementary Benefits Scheme in Great Britain*,
    1978, p. 111.

3 Economic policy 1964-70

1   Robert Bacon and Walter Eltis, *Britain's Economic Problem: Too
    Few Producers*, 2nd edn, Macmillan, 1978, p. 35.
2   Ibid. p. 52.
3   Ibid. p. 51.
4   F.W.S. Craig (ed.), *British Election Manifestos, 1900-1974*, Mac-
    millan, 1975, p. 259.
5   Ibid. pp. 259-60.
6   Harold Wilson, *Purpose in Power: Selected Speeches by Harold
    Wilson*, Weidenfeld & Nicolson, 1966, p. 52.
7   Craig, op. cit., p. 260.
8   Wilson, op. cit.
9   Bacon and Eltis, op. cit., p. 42-3.
10 Department of Employment, *British Labour Statistics, Year Book
    1971*, HMSO, 1972, Table 153.
11 'Joint Statement of Intent on Productivity, Prices and Incomes',
    The Times, 17 December 1964, paras 9 and 10.
12 *British Labour Statistics, Year Book 1971*, op. cit., Table 153.
13 Richard Crossman, *The Crossman Diaries: Selections from the
    Diaries of a Cabinet Minister, 1964-1970*, Hamilton & Cape, 1979,
    p. 199.
14 S. Brittan, 'Inquest on Planning in Britain', *Planning*, no. 499,
    January 1977, p. 23.
15 Central Statistical Office, *National Income and Expenditure,
    1972*, HMSO, 1972, Table 50.
16 *British Labour Statistics, Year Book 1971*, op. cit. Table 153.
17 Ibid.
18 *National Income and Expenditure, 1972*, op. cit., Table 51.
19 'Report on the Conference of Union Executives Held at Croydon
    on 28th February 1968', *T.U.C. Economic Review*, vol. 1, no. 68,
    pp. 6, 88-9.
20 Department of Employment, *Employment Gazette*, October 1972,
    Table 134.

21   J. Leruez, *Economic Planning and Politics in Britain*, trans. Martin
      Harrison, Robertson, 1975, p. 204.
22   H.A. Turner and F. Wilkinson, 'Real Incomes and the Wage Explo-
      sion', *New Society*, 25 February 1971.
23   Central Statistical Office, *Social Trends*, no. 9, HMSO, 1979, Chart
      6.3.
24   C. Jenkins, 'The Jobs Dilemma', *The Times*, 21 October 1968.

4 Economic policy 1970-9

1   Robert Bacon and Walter Eltis, *Britain's Economic Problem: Too
     Few Producers*, 2nd edn, Macmillan, 1978, p. 59.
2   F.W.S. Craig (ed.), *British Election Manifestos, 1900-1974*, Mac-
     millan, 1975, p. 330.
3   Ibid. pp. 329-31.
4   Ibid. pp. 332-3.
5   Ibid. p. 325.
6   Ibid. p. 332.
7   R. Oakley and P. Rose, *The Political Year, 1971*, Pitman, 1971,
     p. 13.
8   J. Leruez, *Economic Planning and Politics in Britain*, trans. Martin
     Harrison, Robertson, 1975, p. 256.
9   Oakley and Rose, op. cit., p. 93.
10 Craig, op. cit., pp. 405-6.
11 H. Wilson, *Final Term: The Labour Government 1974-1976*,
     Weidenfeld & Nicolson, 1979, p. 29.
12 Denis Healey, speech on the economy, *The Times*, 26 February
     1976.
13 Bacon and Eltis, op. cit., p. 132.
14 Stuart Holland, the *Guardian*, 29 May 1980.
15 Central Statistical Office, *National Income and Expenditure, 1979*,
     HMSO, 1979, Table 10.7.
16 Department of Employment, *British Labour Statistics, Year Book
     1976*, HMSO, 1977, Table 57; *Employment Gazette*, January
     1979, p. 37; and *Employment Gazette*, January 1980, p. 34.
17 *British Labour Statistics, Year Book 1976*, op. cit., Table 26; and
     Employment Gazette, January 1980, p. 85, using implied deflators
     of consumers' expenditure from *National Income and Expenditure*
     (1979 edn), Table 2.5.
18 M. Stewart, *Politics and Economic Policy in the U.K. since 1964:
     The Jekyll and Hyde Years*, Pergamon, 1978, p. 241.

5 The new Conservatism

1   Sir Keith Joseph, speech at Preston, *The Times*, 6 September, 1974.
2   F.A. von Hayek, *The Denationalisation of Money*, Institute of

Economic Affairs, 1976, p. 75.
3   *Sunday Times*, 29 June 1980.
4   Ibid.
5   The *Guardian*, 30 June 1980.
6   Ibid., 8 July 1980.
7   Ibid., 12 July 1980.
8   *Sunday Times*, 29 June 1980.
9   The *Guardian*, 11 June 1980.
10 Ibid.
11 *Yesterday in Parliament*, BBC Radio 4, 12 July 1980.
12 Brian Reading, Paul Cockle and Nigel Morgan, 'ITEM Report'
    the *Guardian*, 23 June 1980.
13 Ibid.
14 Ibid.
15 Ibid.
16 The *Guardian*, 24 June 1980.

6 Social policy 1964-70

1   *The National Plan*, Cmnd 2764, 1965, p. 1.
2   C.A.R. Crosland, *The Conservative Enemy*, Cape, 1962, p. 11.
3   D. Jay, *Socialism in the New Society*, Longman, 1962, pp. 222-4.
4   Labour Party, 'New Frontiers in Social Security', 1963, p. 19.
5   R. Crossman, speaking at Labour Party Conference, *Report of the
    59th Annual Conference of the Labour Party, 1960*, p. 103.
6   D. Cole and J. Utting, *The Economic Circumstances of Old People*,
    Codicote, 1962.
7   F.W.S. Craig (ed.), *British Election Manifestos, 1900-1974*, Mac-
    millan, 1975, pp. 265-6.
8   B. Abel-Smith, *Labour's Social Plans*, Fabian Tract 369, 1966, p.5.
9   A. Webb, 'The Abolition of National Assistance', in P. Hall, H.
    Land, R. Parker and A. Webb (eds), *Change, Choice and Conflict*,
    Heinemann, 1975, pp. 450-1.
10 Beveridge, W., *Social Insurance and Allied Services* (the Beveridge
    Report), Cmnd 6404, 1942, paras 23 and 161-3.
11 House of Commons debates, vol. 702, col. 1400, quoted in Webb,
    op. cit., p. 457.
12 A.B. Atkinson, *Poverty in Great Britain and the Reform of Social
    Security*, Cambridge Universtiy Press, 1969, p. 75.
13 House of Commons debates, vol. 704, cols 331-2, quoted in Webb,
    op. cit., p. 455.
14 B. Abel-Smith and P. Townsend, *The Poor and the Poorest*, Bell,
    1965.
15 F. Field, 'A Pressure Group for the Poor', in D. Bull (ed.), *Family
    Poverty*, Duckworth, 1971, p. 152.
16 T. Lynes, 'Clawback', in D. Bull, op. cit., pp. 130-3.
17 D. Wedderburn, 'How Adequate are Our Cash Benefits? ', *New*

Society, vol. 10, no. 263, 12 October 1967, pp. 512-16.

18 F. Field, in D. Bull, op. cit., pp. 149, 153.

19 'Poverty and the Labour Government', *Poverty Pamphlet*, no. 3, Child Poverty Action Group, 1970.

20 T. Lynes, 'The Failure of Selectivity', in D. Bull, op. cit., pp. 21-2.

21 R. Titmuss, *Commitment to Welfare*, Allen & Unwin, 1968, p. 135.

22 M. Meacher, 'The Politics of Positive Discrimination', in H. Glennester and S. Hatch (eds), *Positive Discrimination and Inequality*, Fabian Research Series, no. 314, 1974, p. 5.

23 Ibid.

24 J. Barnes, 'A Solution to Whose Problem? ', in Glennester and Hatch (eds), op. cit., pp. 10-11.

25 Longford, F., *Crime: A Challenge to Us All* (the Longford Report). Report of a Labour Party study group, 1964.

7 Social policy 1970-9

1 Central Statistical Office, *National Income and Expenditure*, HMSO (1952 and 1979 edns), Tables 1.1 and 7.1.

2 I. Gough, *The Political Economy of the Welfare State*, Macmillan, 1979, p. 79.

3 Central Statistical Office, *National Income and Expenditure, 1979*, op. cit., Table 9.4.

4 Ibid.

5 Ibid.

6 Ibid.

7 Gough, op. cit., p. 85.

8 Robert Bacon and Walter Eltis, *Britain's Economic Problem: Too Few Producers*, 2nd edn, Macmillan, 1978, p. 28.

9 Central Statistical Office, *National Income and Expenditure, 1979*, op. cit., Tables 7.1 and 7.4.

10 H. Glennester (ed.), *Labour's Social Priorities*, Fabian Research Series, 327, Fabian Society, 1976, p. 8.

11 D. Bull (ed.), *Family Poverty*, Duckworth, 1971, p. 153.

12 Sir Keith Joseph, 'The Next Ten Years', *New Society*, 5 October 1972.

13 Sir Keith Joseph, speech to Pre-School Playgroup Association, 29 June 1972.

14 Sir Keith Joseph, 'The Next Ten Years', op. cit.

15 Sir Keith Joseph, introducing the second reading of the Family Income Supplements Bill in the House of Commons, *The Times*, 11 November 1970.

16 Department of Health and Social Security, *Children in Care of Local Authorities at 31st March 1972*, HMSO.

17 Denis Healey, introducing the Budget in the House of Commons, April 1975.

18 *The Government's Expenditure Plans*, Cmnd. 6393, 1976, p. 2.

19 *The Government's Expenditure Plans*, Cmnd. 6721, 1977, p. 11.
20 Department of Health and Social Security, *Social Assistance, A Review of the Supplementary Benefits Scheme in Great Britain*, 1978, p. 111.
21 Ibid., p. 11.

8 Social control

1 Sir Keith Joseph, speech on morals, the *Guardian*, 21 October 1974.
2 N. Parton, 'The Natural History of Child Abuse: A Study in Social Problem Definition', *British Journal of Social Work*, vol. 9, no. 4, 1980.
3 A. Shearer, 'Tragedies Revisited, 3', *Social Work Today*, 23 January 1979.
4 O. Stevenson and C. Hallett, 'Case Conferences', Universtiy of Keele, 1977, quoted in A. Shearer, op. cit.
5 J. Packman, *The Child's Generation*, Blackwell and Robertson (2nd edn) 1981, Chapter 9.
6 Ibid.
7 Ibid.
8 Ibid.
9 Ibid.
10 P. Cawson, 'Young Offenders in Care', DHSS Social Research Branch, 1978.
11 S. Millham, R. Bullock and K. Hosie, *Locking Up Children*, Saxon House, 1978.
12 J. Paley, C. Green and D. Thorpe, 'Collision or Collusion', University of Lancaster, Centre for Youth, Crime and Community, 1979.
13 *Express and Echo*, 25 February 1980.

9 The new Conservatives and social policy

1 I. Gough, *The Political Economy of the Welfare State*, Macmillan, 1979, p. 97.
2 C. Cockburn, *The Devil's Decade*, Sidgwick & Jackson, 1973, p. 80.
3 The *Guardian*, 1 August 1980.

10 Alternative futures

1 Karl Marx, *Capital: A Critique of Political Economy* (1877), Everyman Edition, Dent, 1930, p. 456.
2 Ibid., p. 414.
3 Ibid., p. 714.

4 Ibid., p. 474.
5 Ibid.
6 Ibid., p. 477.
7 Ibid., p. 480.
8 Ibid., p. 695
9 Ibid., p. 713.
10 Ibid., p. 712.
11 C.H. Feinstein, *Statistical Tables of National Income, Expenditure and Output of the U.K., 1855-1965*, Cambridge University Press, 1972, Table 7.
12 Ibid., Table 20.
13 Ibid., Tables 21, 17.

Index

Abel-Smith, Brian, 113-14, 118
abuse: child, 146, 153-5; of social
   security system, 117, 140, 144,
   152, 157
agriculture: British, 18-19; employment in, 23, 28-33
Atkinson, A.B., 116
automation, absolute, 35, 38, 42,
   47, 49, 53, 97, 173-4, 178-9

Bacon, Robert, 7, 25-32, 59-70, 78-80,
   87-8, 96-7, 131
balance of payments, 45, 60-1, 62,
   67-8, 75, 85-6, 92, 93, 109, 114
bankruptcies, 96, 98
Barber, Anthony, 77-8
barter, 39-40, 42
Belgium, 46
Benn, Tony, 86
Beveridge, Lord, 47, 49, 76, 116,
   133, 142, 145
Brazil, 102, 179
Brittan, Sam, 67
Brown, George, 61-2, 65, 67

Callaghan, James, 67, 87, 88, 92,
   162, 179
Canada, 125
catering, 5, 7
child abuse, *see* abuse
child benefits, 54, 84-5, 118-20, 133,
   137, 143, 151, 165, 183
child care, 118, 122, 145, 153-6
Child Poverty Action Group, 118-20,
   113
Children and Young Persons Act
   (1963), 135, 152

Children and Young Persons Act
   (1969), 155-6
Children's departments, 122
Chrysler, 86
Cole, D., 112
Colins, M., 23
Community Development Projects,
   121
Confederation of British Industries,
   78, 82
Conservative governments: (1959-
   64), 62, 110-11; (1970-4), 42-3,
   45-6, 77-84, 124-36, 148-9, 162;
   (1979-), 51-3, 96-105, 161-7
Conservative Party, 91, 149-151
Cousins, Frank, 70
Crosland, Anthony, 111
Crossman, Richard, 67, 111, 123
cycle of deprivation, 121, 134-6, 146

Debré, M., 23
de-industrialisation, 28, 31-2, 104-5
Denmark, 46
devaluation, 60, 62, 67, 70, 75
disabled, 84, 141, 172
divorce, 151-2
Donnison, David, 139
Douglas, Major C.H., 182

earnings-related benefits, 112-17,
   136-7, 143
Economic Affairs, Department of,
   63, 65, 70
education: comprehensive, 110;
   expenditure on, 46, 113, 125-31
Educational Priority Areas, 121
elderly, 110-17, 129-30, 145

194

election manifestos: Labour (1964), 61-5, 112-13; Conservative (1970), 80-1; Labour (1974), 84-5, 137
Eltis, Walter, 7, 25-32, 59-70, 78-80, 87-8, 96-7, 131
Employment Act (1980), 97
Ennals, David, 120
European Economic Community, 24, 46, 132, 140

family allowances, *see* child benefits
family breakup, 143-4, 147, 151-3
Family Income Supplements, 133-6
Finer Report, 54, 139, 151-2
Ford Motor Company, 102, 105
France: child benefits in, 151; economic growth in, 14, 21-3, 24, 27-32; social expenditure in, 125; social security in, 46
Friedman, Milton, 15, 43-4, 88, 165

Galbraith, J.K., 15, 174
Germany: economic growth in, 19, 21-2, 24, 27-32; social expenditure in, 125, 174; social security in, 46
Glasgow, 100
Green, C., 156

Hallett, Christine, 154
Hayek, F.A. von, 44, 98-9
Healey, Denis, 86, 88, 92, 138-9
Heath, Edward, 81, 88, 93
Heath government, *see* Conservative governments
Holland, Stuart, 88
Hordern, Peter, 83
Houghton, Douglas, 114-15
housing, 45, 84, 113, 125-9
Howe, Geoffrey, 88, 101
Hume, David, 15
Hunger Marches, 168

income guarantee, 112-16
Industrial Expansion Act (1968), 74, 81
industrialising countries, 24-5
Industrial Reorganisation Corporation, 74, 81
Industrial Training Boards, 74
investment: as a factor in economic growth, 15-20, 35; failure of in Britain, 26-7, 60-4, 68-72, 78; government priority for, 138-9;

rates of in other countries, 27-30
Ireland, 32-3, 35
Italy: economic growth in, 28-32; social expenditure in, 125; social security in, 46

Japan: economic growth in, 5, 14, 24, 27-32, 33, 35, 101; social expenditure in, 124, 174
Jay, Douglas, 111
Jenkins, Clive, 74
Johnson, Lyndon, 121
Joseph, Sir Keith: on employment and monetary policy, 83, 95, 96-7, 101-3; on population, 23, 96; on social policy, 134, 145, 148-9
juvenile delinquency, 122, 144-5, 147, 150, 153, 155-6

Kennedy, John, 121
Keynes, J.M., 40-4, 98-9, 178-9
Keynesian school, 3, 42-4, 86, 88, 93, 96-100, 162

Labour governments, 51, 53-4; (1964-70), 26-27, 45, 59-76, 109-23; (1974-9), 84-91, 134-41, 150, 161-4
labour movement, 53, 168, 170, 179
Labour Party, 53-4, 87, 91, 179
Leruez, Jacques, 71-2
Liechtenstein, 32-3, 35
Lloyd, Ian, 103
Longford Report, 122
low-income families, 110, 118-20, 133-6

Macdonald, Ramsay, 168
maladjustment, 134
Malthus, Thomas, 41
manpower policies, 64, 66, 92
Manpower Services Commission, 92
Marshall, Michael, 102
Marx, Karl, 175-81
Meacher, Michael, 121
means-tested benefits, 47, 110-12, 115, 120, 123, 125, 133-6, 139-42, 146, 167-9, 172
mental health services, 122
microelectronics, 3, 4, 12, 47-8, 102-3
Mill, John Stuart, 20, 40, 41, 174
miners, 82, 89

mining, 71-2, 89
monetarism, 3, 35, 43-4, 46, 52,
    86, 88, 93-4, 96-105, 161-7, 185
Monopolies Commission, 74

National Assistance, 49, 110-17,
    118-19, 141
National Economic Development
    Council, 62
National Enterprise Board, 85
National Health Service, 46, 113,
    125-9
National Insurance: benefits, 50-1,
    111-16, 141, 165-6; contributions,
    9-10, 72-3, 132
National Plan (1965), 61, 64-8, 109-10
National Unemployed Workers Move-
    ment, 168-9
Netherlands, 46, 132
Northern Ireland, 33
North Sea Oil, 84, 88

Organisation for Economic Co-
    operation and Development, 125,
    130

Packman, Jean, 154-5
Paley, J., 156
paternalism, 145-56, 165
pensions, 84-5, 111-14, 136-7, 163
Pensions and National Insurance,
    Ministry of, 115
personal social services: expenditure
    on, 46, 127-9; reform of, 122-3;
    responsibilities of, 135, 147
Place of Safety Orders, 154-5
planning; 61-2, 67, 70, 75; agreements,
    85; document, 69
Plowden Report, 121
Poor Law, 17, 47, 116, 142, 145,
    148, 178
population: in France, 21-3; in
    Germany, 22; in USA, 22; growth
    of, 15-17, 20-3, 33, 129-30
positive discrimination, 120-1
Powell, Enoch, 23, 83
prescription charges, 110, 113
Prices and Incomes Board, 81
productivity deals, 54, 72, 74, 101,
    110, 181-2
Public Sector Borrowing Require-
    ment, 83, 103, 171
public spending: control of, 86, 171-2;

and Heath government, 78-84;
    and Keynesian theory, 40, 42,
    45-7; and social policy, 51, 124-9

rate rebates, 120
Rayner Committee, 166
rent rebates, 135
resource spending, 125-9
'Responsibility in Welfare', 157
Ricardo, David, 14-19, 20, 25, 35,
    41, 99, 175-81
'Ricardo phenomenon': and class
    conflict, 162-4, 174-5; and Con-
    servative governments, 77-8; and
    Keynesian policies, 41-2; and
    Labour governments, 87-90; and
    monetarism, 96-100; onset of,
    37, 59-61, 75; in the 1930s, 184
robots, 47-8, 54, 102
Rolls Royce, 81, 83

Seebohm Report, 122
Selective Employment Tax, 72
Selsdon Conference (1970), 95
silicon chip, 12, 47, 184
single-parent families, 50, 54, 139, 151
Smith, Adam, 15
Social Contract, 84-5, 136-7
social control, 142-58
social dividend, 181-4
social security, 39, 46, 110-20, 125-42,
    165-7, 172
Social Security Act (1980), 152, 166
social wage, 46, 137-8, 142, 182
social workers, 144, 147, 153, 185
socialism, 53, 62, 80, 84-6, 111,
    113, 181-5
Stevenson, Olive, 154
Stewart, Michael, 91, 93
supplementary benefits: 47, 49-50;
    creation of, 114-18; reform of,
    139-42, 150, 166, 171, 183;
    staffing in, 144
supplementation of wages, 43, 133-5,
    146
Sweden, 125, 174

Taiwan, 102, 179
taxation: on consumption, 132-3;
    credits, 166; cuts in, 78, 80, 138;
    increases in, 72-4, 86
Technology, Ministry of, 63, 70, 74
textiles, 10, 20, 71-2

Thatcher, Margaret, 83, 88, 96, 100, 162-4, 171
Thorpe, David, 156
Titmuss, Richard, 120-1
Townsend, Peter, 114, 118
Trade, Board of, 70
Trade and Industry, Department of, 70
trade unions: and prices and incomes, 70-4, 76, 82-3; and productivity, 64-5, 75-6; and Social Contract, 84-5, 136-8; and social policy. 53, 54, 110, 145; and social security cuts, 157, 166, 169-71, 172; and unemployment, 168
Trades Union Congress, 70, 74, 82, 86
transfer payments, 124-33, 165-7, 172, 181-4
Turner, H.A., 72-3, 76

underdeveloped countries, 24-5

United States: economic growth in, 19, 21-3, 27-32; productivity and earnings in, 43-4; social expenditure in, 121, 124-5
universal benefits, 47, 54, 133, 136-7, 139, 141-2
Upper Clyde Shipbuilders, 81
Urban Programme, 121
Utting, J., 112

Varley, Eric, 86

war: effects of, 19, 184-5; in Germany, 24
Webb, Adrian, 114
Welfare Departments, 122
widows, 120
Wilkinson, F., 72-3, 76
Wilson, Harold, 3, 62, 63, 67, 85-6, 92, 161
work-sharing, 54, 182

For Product Safety Concerns and Information please contact our EU
representative GPSR@taylorandfrancis.com
Taylor & Francis Verlag GmbH, Kaufingerstraße 24, 80331 München, Germany